85

ASHKHAIN'S
SAUDI COOKING
OF TODAY

The Author
Ashkhain Skipwith, who is of Armenian origin, was born in the Middle East. Her love of cooking and her culinary skill were inherited from her mother, herself an exceptional cook.
  Since 1972, Ashkhain, who is married, has been living and cooking in Jeddah, Saudi Arabia.

Editorial
Martin Caiger-Smith
John Blackett-Ord

Design
Keith Savage
David Cringle

Illustration
Ahmad Mowaffy
David Cringle (cover)

Ashkhain's Saudi Cooking of Today
Published by Stacey International
128 Kensington Church Street
London W8 4BH
Telex: 298768 STACEY G

© Ashkhain Skipwith 1986.

ISBN 0905743 42 3

Set in Linotronic Plantin by SX Composing Ltd, Essex, England
Printed and bound by Bournehall Press, England.

Acknowledgements
Many people have helped me to prepare this book, directly and indirectly, and my gratitude to all of them is equal. They know who they are, but particular mention must be made of Layla Abdulkader Al-Saleh al-Fadel and her family, and Balqees Balkhayr, who have given me the Saudi cooking of many well-known dishes that I have cooked with a possible Turkish, Lebanese or Syrian influence. I must also mention my husband Patrick whose unrelenting support has made this book possible.

ASHKHAIN'S
SAUDI COOKING
OF TODAY

Ashkhain Skipwith

STACEY
INTERNATIONAL

CONTENTS

For my goddaughters Miranda, Marwenna, Liza, and Sapna.
May they be spared the horrors of 'fast food'.

INTRODUCTION

T HE DESERT KINGDOM of Saudi Arabia stretches from the Red Sea in the west to the
Arabian Gulf, and from Jordan and Iraq in the north to the mountainous Oman and the
Yemens. It encompasses the ancient spice routes from southern Arabia, the fabled gold mines of
King Solomon, and is the centre of Islam through its guardianship of the holy cities of Makkah and
Madinah. Beyond the scattered oases, date gardens and small agricultural settlements, the
traditional way of life was, until recently, bedouin with, of necessity, a sparse cuisine of mutton,
rice and milk, or chicken and rice, or fish and rice . . . with little variation in cooking methods. But
these traditional ways have changed – insularity is no longer possible with the car, the aeroplane,
the refrigerated truck, excellent roads and communications and abundant foreign expertise and
labour bringing with them the benefits of the twentieth century.

The change has been extremely rapid. As recently as fifteen years ago, when I came to live in the
country, it was common to see a Bedouin herding his sheep, goats or camels, riding on a camel
himself. Now one is more likely to see a whole herd of goats, or even a large camel sitting in the
back of a 'pick-up' with the Bedouin at the wheel. Then, the desert was dotted with black camel-
hair tents and the Bedouin cooked on fires of brushwood gathered from the *wadis* – now there are
clusters of white 'Pakistani' tents, and cooking on gas-fed stoves. Visiting a Bedouin encampment
fifteen years ago, one would be offered dried camel- or sheep-milk biscuits (gritty and sour – very
much an acquired taste). Today one would expect wrapped biscuits and a can of Pepsi. Tradition,
however, has by no means died – it has merely been adapted. The Bedouin still eats his home-made
milk biscuits, only offering his guests imported delicacies as a sign of respect. Bakers continue to
bake bread in traditional ovens, but use gas rather than wood. Gas is clean, easily available, and
leaves no ashes.

In the towns, as in towns all over the world, the cuisine has always been more sophisticated. For
centuries it has been enriched by the passing caravans of pilgrims coming for the Hajj, and their
dishes have been adopted by Saudi families and changed to suit their particular circumstances and
tastes. It is here that I have found Saudi cooking to be an exciting and exquisite experience, and it
is on this aspect of Saudi cooking that I have based this book.

Part of the excitement of Saudi cooking, I find, is in the shopping. Although most of the
ingredients, from the freshest fruits to tinned and frozen foods, breads, cakes, sweets and spices,
are now available in the super-airconditioned, canned-music supermarkets, where shopping is the
same the world over, it is the *souks* (markets) that give me the atmosphere, the impetus and the
interest. There you bargain over every kilo of food, not because prices are unreasonable, but
because bargaining is expected. The souk vendors are authentic, kind and humorous. Once I was
looking desperately for fresh beetroots in the vegetable souk. By the time I had got to the end of the
first row of stalls, the whole souk was echoing the word *shamandar* (beetroot). They were out of
season and everyone thought it very funny, but from somewhere the *shamandar* were miraculously
produced by the only vendor who had a whole sack of them; how then could I buy only one kilo? I
bought five kilos, and discovered the art of freezing beetroot. But there is generally little to be

gained price-wise from shopping in the souk for vegetables and fruit. There is indeed little variation in prices unless one buys full boxes of oranges, tomatoes or apples, and the supermarkets are more convenient for those with either transport or language problems (for few in the souk speak English).

Spices, however, are quite a different matter. No supermarket carries the truly Saudi cooking herbs and spices, and those that are available come in tiny bottles or jars, imported, expensive, and unexciting. In the spice souks, they are sold by the kilo and that's the way I prefer it. Nor does the supermarket sell fish, though in Saudi Arabia a large variety of fresh fish is available almost all year round along the coasts. The fish market (*souk as samak*) can be romantic, but in Jeddah it is located downtown and one has to be there very early in the morning to be sure of really fresh fish. Fortunately, there are now some impeccably clean and extremely well-stocked fish shops; shrimps, prawns and crayfish are at their best, moderately priced and, I dare say, they cost not a *halala* more than those in the fish souk. This is one area where logic should prevail over romanticism. As for meat, it should be bought from the supermarket or air-conditioned 'steak house'. Meat in the souk is sold 'on the hoof', whilst in the older, local shops one cannot be sure of the quality.

In common with peoples the world over, the Saudis eat three main meals a day. Food is cooked and served in a rather lavish style and in large quantities, with the full variety of dishes (meat, poultry, pastry, fruit) all served together, whether it is a normal family occasion or a party banquet. Bread is served with every meal at all times, the most popular being *khubz* (round, flat bread). Tea, already sweetened in small glasses, is on hand throughout the day, as is Turkish coffee. Arabic coffee is normally taken before a meal. In addition, every Saudi table sports a small bowl of chilli pepper (ground or whole), *duggus* (a peppery salad, but a must), *jarjeer* (a sharp and tasty type of cress), spring onions, and lemon wedges.

Saudis in the more traditional homes breakfast on tea, *foul madammas*, honey and *gishta* (cream, or top of the milk), cheese, jam and eggs. Before this (or perhaps after) they may take dates and Arabic coffee, possibly accompanied by the perfumed aroma of a small incense burner. The men breakfast early, after morning prayers; the rest of the family eat later in the morning. Lunch, served between one and three in the afternoon, is a large meal, and very much a family occasion, with the children home from school and the father from work. Dinner, again, is large, and often eaten as late as ten o'clock. It may be a family occasion, with parents, children, brothers and their wives, and grandparents, all of whom share a house or (more recently) a family compound. If guests are present, however, the women eat separately.

A banquet may be held to celebrate special occasions such as a wedding, a birth, or the presence of an honoured guest. These are all-male or all-female affairs and truly reflect the renowned Arab hospitality. I have been to several Saudi weddings and to dinner parties given by Saudi ladies. The food is always lavish, but alas, wedding dinners are not served until around three o'clock in the morning, and only after this are guests expected to make a departure. Male gatherings are far less strenuous; whether at a house, a hotel or a banquet hall, the men eat promptly and leave the dining area without much delay.

Saudis seldom eat out, unless they are bachelors, travelling or on business. Travellers stop at midday to eat a picnic lunch or use the road-side restaurants where there are facilities for washing, tea, coffee and cold drinks. If the travellers are all male, they eat indoors, where meat, chicken and rice are generally available. But the road-side restaurants are most frequented in the evenings, when their high *kursi* benches double as open-air beds. When travelling to Riyadh, Najran and Tabuk by car, I often used these road-side restaurants and truly enjoyed the food, though being a woman I was asked to sit in a quiet corner, or outside where I would be really well hidden. I have also eaten in what are called *Mata'im Sha'biyyah* – restaurants serving local cuisine – in various towns, where my only complaint was that the servings were huge.

Places to eat out in the towns and cities are fast developing; as well as the numerous first-class hotels, there are many really top-class establishments serving Arabic, Turkish, Italian, Korean, Indonesian, Chinese and Indian food. Tradition remains, however, in that all, without exception, have 'men only' and 'family only' sections. Some Saudi families frequent these in the evenings, often bringing a large party including children; but more often they are used for business meetings.

The latest foreign intrusion is the advent of 'fast food'. This is not entirely new to Saudi Arabia: *shawerma* and *falafil* stands have been popular for many years. But westernised fast-food – hamburgers and pizzas – and stand-up bars have indeed arrived, with a vengeance. They have sprung up everywhere; one sees them near new housing complexes, in shopping centres, and in the souks. Another newcomer, this time of Arab origin, is the juice shop where exquisite fruits like melon, pomegranate, banana, orange and lemon are freshly squeezed and served. In preparing this book on 'Saudi' cooking, I have excluded, as far as possible, Western influences and concentrated on the Arabic meals of recent years. I have talked, cooked, and eaten with Saudi ladies, and learnt much from them, but the recipes here remain my own, for it is nearly impossible (and with good reason) to find three people agreeing on the exact quantities, contents and order of preparation of each dish. I have myself tested each recipe, modifying the ingredients to make the dish more palatable to my own taste. There are bound to be criticisms of some of the proportions I use; to these I can only say that the dishes do work in the ways I have described them, and have been sampled and approved by gourmets and gourmands alike. However, if you already have an acquired taste for a particular recipe, then it is easy to adjust the herbs, spices and amounts of liquids added, according to your own preferences. If the recipe is new to you, then take my word for it, try it my way and make your adjustments another time. Remember that in Saudi Arabia, as all over the Middle East, meat is cooked, and cooked well – no rare or medium-rare steaks are acceptable. Bear this in mind when I recommend that a meat dish be cooked for two hours or more.

The weights used here are kilos and grams, as used in Saudi Arabia, but for measures I have tended to use cups (American 6 ounces), tablespoons and teaspoons, as well as the more flexible 'by eye' and 'to taste'.

Ashkhain Skipwith, Jeddah, 1985

STARTERS AND SALADS

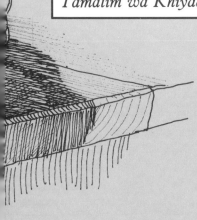

Badhinjan bi Laban	AUBERGINE AND YOGHURT SALAD
Bagdunis bi Tahina	PARSLEY WITH TAHINA
Burak bi Jibin	CHEESE PIE
Burak bi Sabaanikh	SPINACH PIE
Duggus	TOMATO AND CORIANDER SALAD
Fattush	SALAD WITH BREAD
Hummus bi Tahina	CHICK PEA DIP
'Ijjah bi Basal	EGGS WITH ONION
'Ijjah bi Kousa	EGGS WITH COURGETTE
Kousa bi Laban	COURGETTE AND YOGHURT SALAD
Laban bi Khiyaar	YOGHURT AND CUCUMBER
Mutabbal	AUBERGINE DIP
Sabaanikh bi Tahina	SPINACH WITH TAHINA
Salatat al Mukh	BRAIN SALAD
Salatat Badhinjan	AUBERGINE SALAD
Sambousik bi Lahim	MEAT PASTIE
Taboullah	CRACKED WHEAT SALAD
Tamatim bi Tahina	TOMATO SALAD WITH TAHINA
Tamatim Matbukh	COOKED TOMATO SALAD
Tamatim wa Khiyaar	TOMATO AND CUCUMBER SALAD

BADHINJAN BI LABAN

AUBERGINE AND YOGHURT SALAD

A salad usually served in large quantities, together with other cold or hot dishes, at large gatherings.

for four people
2 large aubergines (the plump meaty type)
2 cloves of garlic (crushed)
1 cup of yoghurt (see p. 144)
a few sprigs of parsley
salt
powdered chilli pepper

preparation
1 prick the aubergines in several places with a fork and bake whole over a charcoal fire (or in an oven) until the skins are well charred and the aubergine flesh is soft when pricked with a pointed knife
2 allow to cool, then completely peel the charred skin from the flesh
3 divide the peeled aubergines lengthwise into four pieces, and arrange on a serving platter
4 sprinkle with salt and powdered chilli pepper to taste
5 stir the crushed garlic into the yoghurt and pour evenly over the prepared aubergines
6 decorate with sprigs of parsley

to serve
■ serve cold to accompany meat and vegetable dishes, or kebabs

BAGDUNIS BI TAHINA

PARSLEY WITH TAHINA

This mix makes a perfect sauce or side dish for baked, fried, or poached fish dishes that would otherwise be fairly bland.

for four to six people
3 tablespoons of tahina
juice of 1-2 lemons
4 cloves of garlic (crushed)
1 large bunch of fresh parsley (chopped medium
    to fine)
salt and cayenne pepper

preparation
1   put the tahina into a deep bowl, then
2   slowly add most of the lemon juice, stirring all the time to stabilize the tahina and to stop it
    becoming lumpy – leave some of the lemon juice to add at the end if necessary
3   still stirring, add 2-3 tablespoons of water to thin the tahina
4   then add the crushed garlic, and salt and cayenne pepper to taste
5   add the chopped parsley, and mix well – taste for lemon, salt and pepper

to serve
■ serve with plain fish dishes

CHEESE PIE

Accompanied by tomato salad, olives, and pickles, this makes a very satisfying light lunch.

for six people
dough (see below)
400 grams of white salted (*feta*) cheese
10 spring onions (finely chopped including the
    green parts)
1 cup of fresh parsley (finely chopped)
cayenne pepper
flour
1 egg (beaten)

preparation
1   prepare a *burak* dough according to the recipe '*Ajeenat Sambousik wa Burak* (p. 113) and leave to rest
2   crumble the white cheese into a bowl
3   add the chopped spring onion, chopped parsley, and cayenne pepper to taste, and mix well
4   grease two 20-cm diameter baking trays (or equivalent) and dust with a little flour
5   roll out the dough quite thinly, and cut out linings and lids for the trays
6   line the baking trays with the dough, and spread evenly and thickly with the cheese mixture
7   cover with the dough lids and, with your fingers, stick the edges of the linings and lids together
8   brush the top with beaten egg and prick in several places with a fork to allow steam to escape
9   cook in a pre-heated oven (400°F) for 20-25 minutes, or until the top is golden brown

to serve
■ remove the *burak* from the tray by turning it upside down, then place it the right way up on a plate
■ cut into portions
■ serve hot or cold, though it is best hot

SPINACH PIE

A very suitable dish for picnics, a filler-in at large gatherings, or a main course in a vegetarian meal with cheeses and salads.

for four to six people
dough (see p. 113)
2 bunches of spinach
30 grams of butter
1 large onion (finely chopped)
salt and cayenne pepper
2 tablespoons of pine nuts
1 teaspoon of powdered sumac
flour
1 egg (beaten)

preparation
1 prepare a *burak* dough according to the recipe '*Ajeenat Sambousik wa Burak* (p. 113) and leave to rest
2 wash and drain the spinach, remove the hard stalks, and roughly chop the leaves and tender stalks
3 place the chopped spinach in a pan with about 2 cups of lightly salted boiling water, cover, bring to the boil, then
4 allow to simmer for 2-3 minutes, drain in a colander, and leave aside to cool
5 place the chopped onion in a pan of heated butter with salt and cayenne pepper to taste, and sauté for a few minutes
6 add the spinach, pine nuts, and sumac, mix, sauté for a few minutes more, then remove from the heat and stand to cool
7 grease two 20-cm baking trays (or equivalent) and dust with a little flour
8 roll out the dough quite thinly, and cut out linings and lids for the tray
9 line the baking trays with dough and spread evenly with generous helpings of the spinach and onion mixture
10 cover with the dough lids and, with your fingers, stick the edges of the linings and lids together
11 brush the top with beaten egg and prick in several places with a fork to allow steam to escape
12 bake in a pre-heated oven (400°F) for 20-25 minutes, or until the top is golden brown

to serve
■ remove the *burak* from the tray by turning it upside down, then place it the right way up on a plate
■ cut into portions
■ serve hot with cold yoghurt (see p. 144), or serve cold

DUGGUS

TOMATO AND CORIANDER SALAD

A cooked salad that no table should be without, even though this dish is quite peppery. It is eaten sparingly and can be kept in the refrigerator for a few days.

for six people
4 medium-size tomatoes
2 tablespoons of fresh coriander (chopped)
2 chilli peppers (chopped)
1 clove of garlic (chopped)
salt
juice of 1 large lemon

preparation
1   bake the tomatoes over a charcoal fire (or in an oven) until the skins begin to split, then remove and allow to cool
2   peel and mash the cooked tomatoes with a fork and place in a bowl
3   mix the chopped coriander, chopped chilli pepper, garlic, and salt to taste, then pound them together; alternatively pass them through a grinder
4   add the coriander mixture to the mashed tomatoes and mix
5   add the lemon juice and mix

to serve
■ serve with fish, meat and rice

FATTUSH

SALAD WITH BREAD

A traditional salad containing toasted pieces of flat Arabic bread, which can also make an excellent first course or salad. *Rijlah* leaves or shredded lettuce leaves are essential to the recipe.

for six people
1 loaf of flat Arabic bread (toasted and broken
   into pieces) (see p. 115)
2 large fresh tomatoes (chopped)
2 cucumbers (peeled and finely diced)
3 spring onions (finely chopped including green
   parts)
2 cups of *rijlah* leaves (see p. 153) or shredded
   lettuce leaves
1 tablespoon of fresh mint (chopped)
1 bunch of parsley (chopped)
2 cloves of garlic (chopped) [optional]
1 chilli pepper or ½ teaspoon cayenne pepper
salt
juice of 1-2 lemons
3 tablespoons olive oil

preparation
1   mix the chopped tomatoes, cucumbers, spring onions, shredded *rijlah* or lettuce leaves,
    mint, parsley, garlic (if used) and chilli or cayenne pepper in a salad bowl
2   add salt to taste, olive oil, and lemon juice, and mix
3   taste for oil, lemon, salt, etc., and add more if necessary
4   lastly, just before serving, add the toasted bits of Arabic bread and mix briskly

to serve
■ serve immediately while the pieces of Arabic bread are still crisp

CHICK PEA DIP

This is the famous chick pea dip.

for four people
3 cups of chick peas (measured after being
    soaked overnight and then boiled for at least 1
    hour until very tender – or alternatively using
    tinned pre-cooked *hummus*)
¾ cup of tahina
4 cloves of garlic (crushed)
1 chilli pepper (finely chopped) or a pinch of
    cayenne pepper
juice of 1-2 lemons
pinch of cumin powder
6 black olives for decoration
a few parsley leaves for decoration
a few whole chick peas for decoration
2 tablespoons of olive oil
salt

preparation
1   pound the chick peas into a smooth, even paste – or, much easier, liquidise them in a
    blender, using if necessary a little of the tahina and lemon juice to help in liquidising
2   put the *hummus* paste in a deep bowl and slowly add the tahina, mixing all the time
3   add the crushed garlic and salt and chilli (or cayenne) pepper to taste, and mix
4   slowly add the lemon juice, mixing all the time until a whitish creamy paste is formed – taste
    for lemon before it is all added in case there is too much
5   spread evenly on a platter and sprinkle with cumin
6   decorate with olives, parsley, and whole chick peas, and then pour olive oil evenly all over

to serve
■ serve as a dip with warm Arabic bread (see p. 115)
■ serve as a first course
■ serve at buffets with kebab and salads

EGGS WITH ONION

'Ijjah is an omelette-like dish, made either whole to be cut up at the table or in round individual portions as here. It can be eaten hot, warm, or even cold, and is ideal for buffets as well as for picnic lunches; the fillings are numerous. *'Ijjah bi Basal* is one of the simpler versions using parsley and onions; sometimes flour is added to give it more body and baking powder to make it fluffy, but I recommend you use neither.

for four people
6 eggs
3 tablespoons of fresh parsley (chopped)
4-6 young spring onions (finely chopped
   including some of the green parts)
pinch of cayenne pepper
pinch of cumin
salt and black pepper
vegetable oil

preparation
1   break the eggs into a deep bowl and beat well with a fork – it is not necessary to make them fluffy
2   add the chopped parsley, chopped onions, cayenne pepper, cumin, salt and black pepper to taste, and mix well
3   heat a little vegetable oil in a large frying pan, then
4   lower the heat and carefully ladle out the egg mixture (two or three portions at a time depending on the size of pan) to make thick round *'ijjah* of 8-10 cm diameter
5   cook for about 1 minute so that the bottom of the *'ijjah* is just golden brown, then turn over and similarly cook the other side
6   remove from the pan with a spatula and place on kitchen paper to drain off excess oil

to serve
■ serve hot as a starter with slices of fresh tomato and cucumber
■ serve cold, possibly packed for a picnic lunch, with other cold food and flat Arabic bread (see p. 115)

EGGS WITH COURGETTE

Unlike *'Ijjah bi Basal* (see p. 21), this *'ijjah* is probably best made in one piece as it has a thick juicy filling of diced courgettes.

for four people
2-3 small young courgettes
1 small onion (finely chopped)
6 eggs
3 tablespoons of fresh parsley (finely chopped)
pinch of cumin
salt and black pepper
vegetable oil

preparation
1   wash and dry the courgettes, remove the stalks, and peel
2   boil the peeled courgettes for 10 minutes in sufficient salted boiling water to cover, then remove, drain, cool, and dice quite finely
3   sauté the diced courgettes and chopped onion, with cumin and salt and black pepper to taste, in 1 tablespoon of vegetable oil for 2-3 minutes, then remove from heat and leave aside to cool
4   break the eggs into a deep bowl and beat with a fork
5   add the sautéed courgette mixture to the beaten eggs and mix well
6   heat another 2 tablespoons of vegetable oil in a frying pan (approximately 18 cm in diameter), add the egg and courgette mixture, and cook moderately for about 5 minutes
7   flip the *'ijjah* with the aid of two wooden spatulas and cook the other side for another 5 minutes
8   place in a serving platter, and cut into slices

to serve
■ serve hot
■ serve warm or cold with tomato salad

COURGETTE AND YOGHURT SALAD

This is an ideal accompaniment to roast, grilled, or fried meat dishes. It is also a cooling counterpart to hot spicy meals, and contains enough vegetable to make a perfect vegetable side dish.

for six people
6-8 young courgettes
2-3 cloves of garlic (crushed)
1 cup of fresh home-made yoghurt (see p. 144)
salt and cayenne pepper
1 tablespoon of fresh dill (chopped)

preparation
1   wash the courgettes thoroughly, then top and tail them
2   scrape or peel off a very thin layer of the skin, rinse in cold water, then cut in half lengthwise
3   bring a pan of lightly salted water to the boil, drop the courgettes into it, and boil for 8-10 minutes
4   drain the courgettes well, and place them in a circle on a round platter
5   mix the crushed garlic with the yoghurt, add salt and cayenne pepper to taste, and mix well
6   pour the yoghurt mixture over the cooked courgettes
7   sprinkle with dill just before serving

to serve
■ serve as a salad or a cold vegetable dish

YOGHURT AND CUCUMBER

A dish which can be served as a cold soup, as a side dish with pilaffs, or as a sauce to cool hot peppery kebabs. It is best made with home-made yoghurt and garnished with fresh mint.

for four people
2 cups of fresh home-made yoghurt (see p. 144)
4 cucumbers (peeled and finely diced)
1-2 cloves of garlic (crushed)
salt
paprika
1 tablespoon of fresh mint (chopped)

preparation
1   place the yoghurt in a deep bowl and mix with a fork to liquidise
2   add the diced cucumber, salt to taste, and crushed garlic
3   mix well with a fork
4   place in a serving bowl, or divide into four individual bowls, and chill
5   sprinkle with paprika and mint just before serving

to serve
■ serve as a side dish for meat or vegetable dishes

AUBERGINE DIP

The word *mutabbal* means herbed and spiced but is now used commonly for this dish of mashed aubergine and tahina. It is one of the most delicious aubergine dishes and is served as a dip, a starter, or a side dish. Although, like many other dishes given here, its origins are not necessarily Saudi, it now forms part of today's cuisine and this is the way I have eaten it in Saudi homes.

for four people
1 very large aubergine (about ½ kilo of the
   plump meaty type)
3 tablespoons of tahina
salt and cayenne pepper
1-2 cloves of garlic (crushed)
juice of 1-2 lemons
pomegranate seeds (from ½ a pomegranate)
olive oil
paprika
mint for garnish

preparation
1   prick the aubergine in several places with a fork, and bake it whole over a charcoal fire (or in the oven) for about 1 hour, or until its skin is well charred and the aubergine flesh is soft when pricked with a pointed knife
2   allow the aubergine to cool then peel it
3   place the flesh in a deep bowl, and mash it as fine as possible with a potato masher – do **not** put it into a liquidiser
4   add the tahina, salt and cayenne pepper to taste, and crushed garlic, and mix well
5   add the juice of 1 lemon (or more as necessary), and mix thoroughly with a fork
6   spread thickly on a flat platter, and sprinkle with pomegranate seeds, 1 tablespoon or more of olive oil, and some paprika, and garnish with small sprigs of mint

to serve
■ serve as a starter with warm flat Arabic bread (see p. 115)
■ serve with other cold dishes at a buffet

SABAANIKH BI TAHINA

SPINACH WITH TAHINA

A spinach salad dressed with tahina sauce. It is used both as a dip, and as a salad for meat and fish.

for six people
2 bunches of spinach
4-5 tablespoons of tahina
juice of 2 lemons
4 cloves of garlic
2 chilli peppers (finely chopped)
2 tablespoons of olive oil
salt
paprika

preparation
1   wash the spinach thoroughly, and drain
2   remove the hard stalks, then roughly chop the leaves and tender stalks
3   boil about 2 cups of lightly salted water in a pan, add the chopped spinach, cover, bring again to the boil, then
4   allow to simmer for about 8-10 minutes, drain really well in a colander, and leave aside to cool
5   further chop (almost mash) the cooked spinach
6   place the tahina in a serving bowl, and slowly add the lemon juice mixing all the time
7   add the crushed garlic, finely chopped chilli peppers, salt to taste, and mix
8   finally add the spinach and mix really well – if it is too thick, add a little water
9   place the spinach mixture in deep or shallow serving dish
10 just before serving pour the olive oil evenly over the spinach, and sprinkle with paprika

to serve
■ serve as a dip with warm flat Arabic bread (see p. 115)
■ serve as a salad for meat and fish dishes

BRAIN SALAD

Brain salad is an excellent side dish, and an even better starter. However it is usually sampled cautiously by those who have never previously tried it, so it is best made in small quantities when introducing it for the first time.

for four people (to try)
2 lamb's brains
2 ounces of vinegar (grape or apple)
1 small onion (quartered)
1-2 small fresh tomatoes (cut into rings)
1 tablespoon of parsley (chopped)
juice of 1 lemon
1 tablespoon of olive oil
salt and black pepper
6 pitted (stoned) black olives

preparation
1   stand the brain under cold running water for several minutes, then peel the skin using a sharp pointed knife
2   place the washed, peeled brain in a saucepan, add the vinegar, 1 teaspoon of salt, the onion, and cover with cold water
3   bring to the boil, then allow to simmer for 15 minutes – do not let the water completely evaporate
4   remove the pan from the heat and leave aside to let the brains cool in their own juice
5   make a dressing with the lemon juice, olive oil, salt and black pepper, and mix
6   remove the brains from their juice, and drain well, then
7   using a sharp knife, cut them into strips
8   place the strips of brain on a small serving dish and
9   decorate with olives between the strips, and with tomato rings and parsley around the dish
10 pour the lemon and oil dressing all over

to serve
■ serve with warm flat Arabic bread (see p. 115)
■ serve as a starter accompanied by other side dishes

AUBERGINE SALAD

Served with an oil and lemon or oil and vinegar dressing, normally in large quantities along with other cold or hot dishes at large gatherings.

for four people
2 large aubergines (the plump meaty type)
2 tablespoons of olive oil
juice of one lemon (or two tablespoons of
    vinegar)
1 clove of garlic (crushed)
salt and chilli pepper
a few sprigs of parsley
pomegranate seeds (from ½ a small
    pomegranate)

preparation
1 prick the aubergines in several places with a fork, and bake whole over a charcoal fire (or in an oven) until the skin is well charred and the aubergine flesh is soft when pricked with a pointed knife
2 allow to cool, then completely peel the charred skin from the flesh
3 divide the peeled aubergines lengthwise into 4, and arrange on a serving platter
4 make a dressing of the olive oil and lemon juice (or olive oil and 2 tablespoons of vinegar) with the garlic, salt and chilli pepper, mix well, and pour evenly over the cooked aubergines
5 sprinkle with sprigs of parsley and seeds of pomegranate

to serve
■ serve cold as a salad or a side dish with warm flat Arabic bread (see p. 115)

SAMBOUSIK BI LAHIM

MEAT PASTIE

Small pasties served as an appetizer or as 'finger food'. These can be either baked or deep fried, and one person can easily eat 6-8 at a time. This is but one of numerous *sambousik* recipes.

for six people (or 35-40 *sambusiks*)
dough (see p. 113)
½ kilo of beef or lamb (minced)
1 medium sized onion (finely chopped)
2 heaped tablespoons of pine nuts
2 tablespoons of parsley (finely chopped)
vegetable oil
1 beaten egg [if baking]
salt and black pepper
cayenne pepper

preparation
1   prepare a dough according to the *'Ajeenat Sambousik wa Burak* recipe (see p. 113) and allow to rest
2   gently heat the 2 tablespoons of vegetable oil in a pan, add the minced meat and brown for about 10 minutes turning frequently
3   add the chopped onion, salt, black pepper, and cayenne pepper to taste, and continue mixing and browning for a further 10 minutes,
4   add the pine nuts and parsley, and brown for a further 5 minutes, still mixing, then
5   remove from the heat and leave to cool
6   divide the dough into 2 portions, and roll into balls
7   roll out each ball thinly with a rolling pin and, using a round dough cutter (or a large glass upside down), cut out circles approximately 10 cm across
8   place about 1 dessertspoon of the meat mixture on to each dough circle, then
9   wet the rims with water, fold the dough over to form half a bulging circle, and close by pressing down the edges with a fork
10   either deep fry in hot vegetable oil until golden brown **or**
10a place the pasties onto a greased round baking tray, brush the tops with beaten egg, and place in a pre-heated oven (375°F) for about 15 minutes, or until the tops are golden brown

to serve
■ serve hot or cold
■ store in fridge or freezer when cold, re-heat when ready to serve

TABOULLAH

CRACKED WHEAT SALAD

Just about every Middle Eastern country claims *taboullah* as its own. I have tried it the Saudi way, the Lebanese way, the Syrian way, and so on, and finally have come to the happy solution of taking everyone's advice and making it as given here. *Taboullah* is customarily eaten folded daintily in small lettuce or vine leaves, though, if you must, it can be eaten with a fork.

for six people
1 cup of *burghul* (cracked wheat)
4 spring onions (finely chopped, including green
    parts)
4 cucumbers (peeled and finely chopped)
2 cups of fresh parsley (chopped)
1 cup of fresh mint (chopped)
4 red tomatoes (finely chopped)
salt and cayenne pepper
juice of 2 lemons
½ cup of olive oil

preparation
1   contrary to popular belief, do **not** soak the *burghul* or you will have a mushy rather than a crispy *taboullah* – if you wish, you can rinse and then dry the *burghul*
2   place the *burghul* in a deep bowl and add the chopped tomatoes, cucumbers, spring onions, parsley and mint, and mix gently
3   leave for half an hour to allow the *burghul* to absorb the juices
4   add salt and cayenne pepper to taste, and mix
5   add some olive oil, then lemon juice, and mix well
6   taste for lemon, oil, salt, etc., and add more if necessary

to serve
■ serve within 15 minutes of adding the olive oil and lemon juice so that it is not soggy
■ serve on a large platter on a bed of lettuce leaves
■ serve lettuce or vine leaves on the side to eat it with

TAMATIM BI TAHINA

TOMATO SALAD WITH TAHINA

Excellent with both fish and meat dishes, or used as a dip.

for four people
4 medium tomatoes (finely chopped)
2 tablespoons of fresh parsley (chopped)
3 tablespoons of tahina
juice of 1-2 lemons (or vinegar)
2-3 cloves of garlic (crushed)
2 chilli peppers (1 finely chopped; 1 sliced)
salt

preparation
1   place the tahina in a deep bowl
2   slowly add the lemon juice (or vinegar), mixing all the time with a fork to stabilize the tahina
3   add the crushed garlic, the finely chopped chilli pepper and salt to taste, the chopped tomatoes, and the chopped parsley
4   mix very well, but do not totally mush the tomatoes
5   place in a serving bowl and decorate with slices of chilli pepper

to serve
■ serve with warm flat Arabic bread (see p. 115)

COOKED TOMATO SALAD

A peppery salad, normally served in small quantities. It is excellent with plain fish dishes, grilled meats, and with plain rice. It is worth making in double or triple quantities and storing it in the fridge.

for six people
4 ripe tomatoes (peeled and chopped)
2 onions (chopped)
2 cloves of garlic (chopped)
3 chilli peppers (finely chopped)
2 tablespoons of vegetable oil
salt and black pepper

preparation
1   gently heat the vegetable oil in a pan, add the chopped onions, and sauté, stirring constantly, until they are pinkish
2   add the garlic, then the chilli pepper and gently sauté for a few minutes more, still mixing
3   add salt and black pepper to taste, then the chopped tomatoes, and mix
4   cook gently for about 10 minutes, mixing occasionally and making sure it remains juicy
5   remove from the heat and allow to cool

to serve
■ serve cold as a side dish with fish or meat

TAMATIM WA KHIYAAR

TOMATO AND CUCUMBER SALAD

One of the many Arabic salads of tomato and cucumber. It makes a refreshing accompaniment to meat, poultry, or fish dishes.

for four people
4 large fresh tomatoes
4 cucumbers
1 onion
small bunch of fresh mint
small bunch of fresh parsley
juice of 1 large lemon
2 tablespoons of olive oil
salt and ground chilli pepper

preparation
1   wash and dry the vegetables thoroughly, then
2   chop the tomatoes into irregular chunks
3   peel the cucumbers, and cut into quite thick half rings
4   peel the onion, and cut into thin segments, and
5   coarsely chop the leaves of the mint and parsley
6   place the tomatoes, cucumbers, and onion in a deep bowl, and mix
7   add the chopped mint and parsley
8   make a dressing of lemon juice and olive oil, with salt and ground chilli pepper to taste – this can be based on 1 measure of olive oil to 1½ measures of lemon juice
9   add the dressing just before serving

to serve
■ serve with fish, meat or chicken and rice dishes

SOUPS

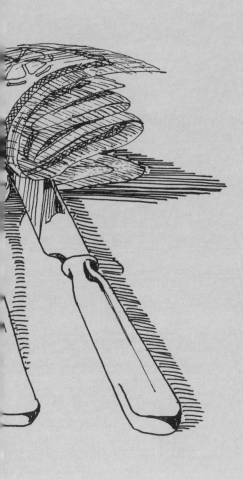

Shorbat 'Adas	LENTIL SOUP
Shorbat 'Adas bi Khudaar	LENTIL AND VEGETABLE SOUP
Shorbat Habb	GRAIN SOUP
Shorbat Kawari'	LAMB TROTTER SOUP
Shorbat Samak	FISH SOUP

SHORBAT 'ADAS

LENTIL SOUP

Made with split red lentils, coriander and parsley.

for four people
1½ cups of red lentils (washed)
1 onion (whole, peeled)
4 cups of stock (beef)
6 cloves of garlic (4 whole, peeled; 2 chopped)
salt and black pepper
50 grams of butter
2 tablespoons of fresh coriander (chopped)
2 tablespoons of fresh parsley (chopped)

preparation
1   boil the lentils in 4 cups of water, then allow to simmer for 30 minutes
2   heat the stock, add it to the lentils, then
3   add the whole onion, the whole cloves of garlic, and salt and pepper to taste, and continue cooking gently for a further 30 minutes
4   liquidize the soup in a blender, then return it to the pan
5   heat the butter, add the chopped garlic, parsley, and coriander, mix, and gently sauté for 2-3 minutes
6   pour the butter, parsley, and coriander mixture into the soup, bring to the boil once, and remove from the heat

to serve
■ serve lemon wedges on the side
■ serve hot with Arabic bread (see p. 115) and turnip pickles (see p. 127)

LENTIL AND VEGETABLE SOUP

A variation of the previous recipe, with the addition of vegetables.

for four people
as for *Shorbat 'Adas* (see opposite)
2 small courgettes (peeled and diced)
2 small carrots (peeled and diced)

preparation
Follow the preparation for *Shorbat 'Adas*, except for step 3, which should be:
3 add the diced vegetables, the whole onion, whole clove of garlic, and salt and pepper to taste, and cook until the courgettes and carrots are very soft

to serve
■ serve as with *Shorbat 'Adas*

SHORBAT HABB

GRAIN SOUP

This is made of whole wheat kernels with their husks removed. It is an exceptionally good soup made by some families throughout the holy month of Ramadan, but it must be planned well in advance as it demands at least 4 hours cooking time.

for eight people
½ cup of *habb* (husked wheat kernels)
½ kilo of lamb (chunks on the bone)
1 stick of cinnamon
½ teaspoon of cumin seeds
5 black peppercorns (whole)
1 piece of *shaiba* (a lichen – see p. 153)
1 piece of *khulinjan* (see p. 152)
4 cardamom seeds (whole)
2 tablespoons of tomato purée
salt

preparation
1   soak the *habb* overnight in cold water, then rinse thoroughly
2   place the *habb* in a large pan with 8 cups of cold water, bring to the boil, then allow to simmer for about 2 hours – add hot water whenever necessary, as the water level must remain above the grain at all times
3   add the chunks of meat, add the cinnamon, cumin, peppercorns, *shaibah*, *khulinjan*, cardamom, tomato purée, and salt to taste, and mix
4   bring to the boil again, then allow to simmer for another 2-3 hours, adding water to keep the soup at your required thickness

to serve
■ serve hot
■ can be re-heated if not used immediately

SHORBAT KAWARIʿ

LAMB'S TROTTER SOUP

Customarily eaten for breakfast on those bone-chilling mornings that one experiences in the heart of the desert. It is a very tasty clear soup; squeeze lots of lemon on top, sprinkle with some paprika, and you have an excellent first course.

for four people
4 lamb's trotters
2 lemons (cut into wedges)
paprika
salt
bouquet of whole spice (tied in gauze)
containing:
    1 piece of *mistika* (see p. 152)
    5 black peppercorns (whole)
    1 piece of *shaiba* (lichen – see p. 153)
    1 stick of cinnamon
    3 cardamom seeds (whole)
    5 cloves (whole)

preparation
1   clean, wash, and pat the trotters dry, then
2   singe the trotters over a naked flame to burn off any hairs left on them, and rinse again thoroughly
3   place the trotters in a pressure cooker (or pan) and add 6 cups of cold water, salt to taste, and the whole spice bouquet
4   cook very well for about 45 minutes in the pressure cooker or for about 2 hours, until the meat is falling off the bone, in the ordinary pan – you may need to add hot water as it evaporates while simmering
5   strain the stock, then
6   pick the meat off the bones, add it to the soup stock, and sprinkle with paprika

to serve
■ serve hot with wedges of lemon to squeeze on soup as desired
■ serve with warm flat Arabic bread (see p. 115) and pickles (see pp. 123-128)

FISH SOUP

This tastes best made with shark or jack fish.

for six people
1 kilo of fish fillets (cut up, boned and skinned)
1 onion (divided in half)
4 cloves of garlic (whole)
1 tablespoon of grape vinegar
1 tablespoon of Worcestershire sauce
50 grams of butter
salt
bouquet of whole spices (tied in gauze)
containing: 6 cloves (whole)
          2 sticks of cinnamon
          6 cardamom seeds (whole)
          2 bits of *mistika* (see p. 152)
          6 peppercorns (whole)

preparation
1   put pieces of fish in enough water to cover, and bring to the boil
2   while it is boiling, add the vinegar, onion, garlic, Worcestershire sauce, and the bouquet of whole spices
3   add the butter, and salt to taste, lower the heat, and allow to simmer until the fish is falling apart
4   strain the stock and return it into the pot (adding more water if necessary)
5   mash or purée the fish, add it to the soup stock, mix, and briskly bring to the boil once

to serve
■ pour into a tureen and serve hot
■ stir before each serving as the puréed fish settles and the clear stock floats

MEAT DISHES

Al Mataziz	LAMB, DUMPLINGS, AND VEGETABLES
Badhinjan Mahshi ma' Laban	STUFFED AUBERGINES WITH YOGHURT
Bamya bi Lahim	LAMB WITH OKRA
Batatis Mahshi	STUFFED POTATOES
Bazella bi Lahim	LAMB WITH GREEN PEAS
Fakhid Kharouf	LEG OF LAMB
Fakhid Kharouf bi Laban	LEG OF LAMB COOKED IN YOGHURT
Fasulyah Baydah	WHITE BEANS WITH BEEF OR LAMB
Fattat Kawari'	LAMB'S TROTTERS
Kabsat Lahim	LAMB AND RICE
Kibda bi Thawm	LIVER WITH GARLIC
Kufta bi Tahina	MINCED BEEF WITH TAHINA
Kufta Kabab	MINCED MEAT KEBAB
Kousa bil Mafroum	COURGETTES WITH BEEF OR LAMB
Lahim wa 'Ajeen	LAMB AND PASTRY
Mahshi Jazar, Lifit, Khiyaar	STUFFED CARROTS, TURNIPS AND CUCUMBERS
Margoug	LAMB WITH THIN BREAD
Mnazzalah	LAMB WITH TAHINA
Saleeq	LAMB AND RICE BOILED IN MILK

LAMB, DUMPLINGS AND VEGETABLES

A lamb and vegetable dish with dough circles cooked in the stock. Not all the vegetables are compulsory; for instance beans can be substituted by peas, and courgettes by gourd or other squash.

for four people

dough (see below)
¾ kilo of lamb (cut into chunks on or off the bone)
2 small aubergines (cut into rings with peel)
3 small courgettes (cut into rings with peel)
3 potatoes (peeled and cut into rings) [optional but good]
12 sticks of green haricot beans (chopped in halves)
4 tomatoes (chopped)
4 small carrots (whole, peeled)

1 tablespoon of tomato pureé
1 large onion (finely chopped)
mixed (whole) cardamom, cloves, *shaiba* (see p. 153)
vegetable oil
3 cloves of garlic (chopped)
1 chilli pepper (chopped)
salt and black pepper
pinch of cumin powder
2 pieces of *mistika* (see p. 152)

preparation

1 make the dough according to the recipe 'Ajeenat al Mataziz (see p. 112), and allow to rest
2 heat about 3-4 tablespoons of oil in a pan, and individually fry to a golden colour, remove, and drain on kitchen paper, first the aubergine rings then the courgette rings, and finally the potato rings (if used)
3 heat 2 tablespoons of oil in a second pan, add the chopped onion and sauté – do not brown – for a few minutes, then add the garlic, and then the meat, and stir
4 add the *mistika* while stirring, and gently brown the meat with the onions and garlic for 10 minutes
5 add the tomato purée, sauté some more, then add the chopped beans followed by the tomatoes, and mix
6 add 4 cups of boiling water, bring to the boil, and allow to simmer for 30 minutes
7 now add the fried vegetables, the small carrots, chilli pepper, salt and black pepper to taste, cumin, and mixed spices, and mix well – you may need to add more boiling water
8 bring all the ingredients to the boil and allow to cook gently for a further 20 minutes
9 meanwhile roll out the dough to a ½ cm thickness and cut out small circles with a biscuit cutter (or upturned glass), using all the dough
10 now briskly bring the meat and vegetables to the boil and drop in the dough circles one by one, allowing them to boil and float; then lower the heat again and cook gently for another 15 minutes – taste a piece of dough and if cooked, remove the pan from the heat

to serve
■ serve hot with plain white rice

BADHINJAN MAHSHI MA' LABAN

STUFFED AUBERGINES WITH YOGHURT

Aubergines filled with meat and pine nuts and served on a bed of thin bread (*ragayig*) and yoghurt.

for six people
12-14 small aubergines
¾ kilo of lamb or beef (minced)
1 large onion (finely chopped)
2 tablespoons of parsley (finely chopped)
2 tablespoons of pine nuts
1 teaspoon of mixed spices (ground)
70 grams of tomato purée
2 cups of yoghurt (see p. 144)
2 cloves of garlic (crushed)
2-4 loaves (depending on size) of thin bread
    (*ragayig*)
butter
salt and black pepper

preparation
1   wash and dry the aubergines, and cut off the stalks
2   core the aubergines with a long thin corer until you are left with thin (½ cm thick) shells, and immerse the shells in cold water
3   heat about 50 gm of butter, add the minced meat, and brown for 10 minutes stirring all the time, then
4   add the onion and continue browning for a further 5 minutes
5   add the parsley, pine nuts, salt and pepper to taste, and the mixed spices, brown for about 10 minutes while stirring, then remove from the heat
6   thoroughly rinse out the cored aubergines, drain all water from them, and fill them with equal amounts of the meat mixture, then
7   place the aubergines in a pan with the open ends upward
8   dilute the tomato purée in 2 cups of water, add a dab of butter, salt and pepper, and pour into the pan with aubergines – see that the level of liquid reaches only about half the height of the aubergines
9   bring quickly to the boil and allow to simmer for about 40 minutes (add boiling water if necessary, so that the pan does not dry up), and remove from the heat when cooked
10 pile the *ragayig* (thin loaves) one on top of the other on a large serving platter
11 add the crushed garlic to the yoghurt, mix, and pour evenly over the *ragayig*, then
12 place the cooked aubergines on top of the yoghurt and bread

to serve
■ serve hot immediately
■ serve the cooking sauce separately on the side

BAMYA BI LAHIM

LAMB WITH OKRA

The vegetable okra, also known as 'ladies' fingers', cooked with lamb and served with rice is a complete main course. Served hot or just warm, it goes quite well with other more meaty dishes or pilaffs when several main dishes are served together.

for four people
½ kilo of *bamya* (okra)
½ kilo of stewing lamb (medium size chunks on
  or off the bone)
2 teaspoons of fresh coriander (chopped), or 1
  teaspoon of dried coriander
1 chilli pepper (chopped)
4 cloves of garlic (peeled, whole)
1 onion (chopped)
6 ripe tomatoes (peeled and chopped)
salt and black pepper
2 lemons
vegetable oil

preparation
1   wash and dry the *bamya*, and cut off the woody tops, being careful not to cut too low and expose the seeds inside
2   sweat the lamb in a pan over a gentle heat, then add about 2 tablespoons of oil and brown it quite well for 10 minutes
3   add the chilli pepper, coriander, garlic, onion, and salt and black pepper to taste, mix, and gently brown for a further 10 minutes, mixing occasionally
4   add the *bamya* and brown it for a few minutes with the meat mixture, still mixing
5   now add the tomatoes, mix, and allow it all to bubble gently for 4-5 minutes
6   add a cup of boiling water, bring to the boil, then allow to simmer gently for about 30 minutes – it must remain juicy, so add a little water if necessary
7   when fully cooked, add the juice of a ½ lemon and remove from the heat

to serve
■ serve hot with plain rice
■ serve lemon wedges on the side

BATATIS MAHSHI

STUFFED POTATOES

There are various stuffings, but all are based on meat and onion, and you have the option of adding walnuts or pine nuts according to taste. This dish can be frozen when cooked and then defrosted and reheated as required.

for four people
½ kilo of lean beef or lamb (coarsely minced)
10-12 small-medium round potatoes
1 large onion (finely chopped)
2 tablespoons of pine nuts or walnuts
2 tablespoons of parsley (chopped)
50 grams of tomato purée
vegetable oil
butter
salt and black pepper

preparation
1 peel the potatoes, core them as you would an apple (leaving about ½ cm thick shell), then rinse them and pat them dry with kitchen paper
2 briefly fry the cored potatoes in oil to seal them, then leave aside on kitchen paper to drain
3 heat about 2 tablespoons of oil in a separate pan, add the meat, the onion, salt and black pepper to taste, and brown gently for about 15 minutes, turning to stop the onion from burning
4 add the nuts and parsley, and brown for a further 5 minutes, still turning all the time, then remove from the heat
5 fill the potatoes with the meat stuffing, and place them in an oven dish with the open ends upward
6 separately dilute the tomato purée in 2 cups of boiling water, add a little salt and pepper, and pour over the stuffed potatoes – do not completely cover the potatoes with liquid
7 cover the dish with a lid or foil, place in a preheated (400°F) oven, and cook for 20 minutes – then uncover and let the potatoes brown for another 5 minutes at a temperature of 300°F.
7a alternatively, place the potatoes in an ordinary pan and cook on a stove by bringing to the boil then allowing to simmer for 45 minutes – but make sure that potatoes are not overcooked and crumbling

to serve
■ serve hot with fresh green salad

BAZELLA BI LAHIM

LAMB WITH GREEN PEAS

This is a quickly prepared meal, served as a main course with plain rice.

for four people
2 cups of green peas (after podding)
½ kilo of stewing lamb (cubed)
70 grams tomato purée, or ½ kilo of fresh
    tomatoes (chopped)
2 tablespoons of fresh coriander (chopped)
2 tablespoons of fresh parsley (chopped)
    [optional]
2 onions (cut into rings)
2 cloves of garlic (chopped)
salt and black pepper

preparation
1   place the onions in the bottom of a greased pan
2   add the lamb on top of the onions, and then add the peas
3   sprinkle with coriander, parsley, garlic, and salt and pepper to taste
4   now place the chopped fresh tomato [if used], **or**
4a dilute the tomato purée in hot water and pour over the layers of vegetables – the liquid must not
    go above the level of the vegetables
5   cover, place on a stove, bring to the boil, then simmer gently for 25-30 minutes, making sure
    that the liquid does not dry up

to serve
■ serve hot with plain rice

LEG OF LAMB

A recipe from southern Saudi Arabia. It was traditionally roasted in the baker's oven or in wood-fired ovens, but is now cooked in gas or electric ovens. Ask your butcher to bone the leg of lamb but to keep the meat in one piece.

for six people
1½ kilos of leg of lamb (after boning, but in one
   piece)
4 tablespoons of olive oil
1 teaspoon of thyme
1 teaspoon of rosemary leaves
1 tablespoon of fresh mint (chopped)
½ teaspoon of cumin seeds
pinch of sugar
2-3 bay leaves
4-6 whole cloves
salt and black pepper

preparation
1   spread out the boned meat with the inside part facing upwards
2   rub on some of the olive oil and sprinkle with salt and pepper
3   mix the thyme with the rosemary leaves, cumin seeds, sugar, and mint, and rub this mixture all over the inside part of the meat
4   place the bay leaves and whole cloves in a row down the middle of the meat, then
5   roll up the meat and tie it with string (as you would for any roast)
6   rub the remaining olive oil on the outside of the rolled meat and sprinkle with salt and pepper
7   place in a lightly greased oven dish and put in a pre-heated oven (425°F) for 10 to 15 minutes,
8   reduce the heat to 350°F and continue cooking for a further 1½ to 2 hours, basting the roast occasionally with its own juice

to serve
■ serve hot with plain rice and a green salad
■ serve warm, sliced and arranged on a serving platter

LEG OF LAMB COOKED IN YOGHURT

The meat is marinated in yoghurt and cooked in the oven.

for six people
1½-2 kilos of leg of lamb (on the bone)
2 cups of yoghurt (see p. 144)
½ cup of tomato juice (from fresh tomatoes)
½ teaspoon of turmeric or saffron
8 cloves of garlic (peeled, whole)
1 teaspoon of mixed ground spices
salt and black pepper
2 tablespoons of olive oil

preparation
1 wash and dry the leg of lamb
2 make 8 small incisions with a pointed knife and insert a whole clove of garlic and a minute touch of salt and black pepper in each cut
3 smear the leg with olive oil
4 mix the yoghurt with the tomato juice, mixed spices, turmeric (or saffron), and a little salt and black pepper, and pour over the meat
5 leave the meat to marinate for 2-4 hours in a cool place, then
6 cover and cook in a pre-heated oven (350°F) for 1½ to 2 hours, basting occasionally with the yoghurt mix

to serve
■ serve hot with plain rice

WHITE BEANS WITH BEEF OR LAMB

A very popular Arabian stew of dried white beans, cooked with lamb or beef and tomatoes, and served with plain white rice accompanied by radishes and spring onions. There are, of course, several variations such as the addition of coriander or parsley, or the use of tomato purée.

for four people
250 grams of white dried haricot beans
¾ kilo of stewing lamb (chunks on the bone) or
  beef (chunks)
1 large onion (chopped into large pieces)
1 chilli pepper (chopped)
8 ripe tomatoes (peeled and chopped)
1 whole head of garlic (washed but unpeeled)
50 grams of butter
salt and black pepper

preparation
1 soak the beans overnight in cold water, then rinse very well
2 place the rinsed beans in a large pan with sufficient cold water to more than cover them
3 bring the beans to the boil, then allow to simmer for at least 1 hour until beans are cooked – add boiling water if necessary
4 meanwhile put the meat chunks into another pan and sweat them over a gentle heat, turning regularly
5 add the butter and, still turning, brown the meat for 10 minutes
6 add the chopped onion and continue browning for another 10 minutes – do not allow the onion to burn
7 add the chopped chilli pepper, and salt and black pepper to taste, and mix all together while still on the heat
8 add the chopped tomatoes, mix, and allow to simmer gently for about 10 minutes to extract the juice of the tomatoes
9 finally drop in the head of garlic and, while the whole mixture is still simmering, add the pan of cooked beans with its liquid and mix thoroughly
10 allow to simmer for 30 minutes, making sure that the liquid does not dry up – add boiling water if necessary

to serve
- serve hot in deep bowls with rice on the side – give the whole head of garlic to the garlic lover
- leftovers keep perfectly well in the fridge for a day or two and can be reheated

LAMB'S TROTTERS

Served with flat Arabic bread, this is an ideal dish for cold weather, such as is experienced in winter in much of Saudi Arabia from where I assume the recipe originated. It is inexpensive, good to taste and, I am sure, good for you.

for four people

4-6 lamb's trotters
1 cup of cooked chick peas
1 loaf of flat Arabic bread (see p. 115)
1 lemon
3-4 cloves of garlic (crushed)
1-2 cups of yoghurt (see p. 144)
salt
1 onion (peeled, whole)

juice of 1 lemon
butter
5 black peppercorns
5 cardamom seeds (whole)
1 cinnamon stick
1 bit of *mistika* (see p. 152)
1 piece *shaiba* (see p. 153)

preparation

1 wash and thoroughly clean the trotters (they are rubbed with salt and flour to remove all slime), and then dry them
2 singe the trotters lightly over a naked flame to burn off any hairs that may be left, then
3 rub them well with lemon wedges, and rinse
4 place the trotters in a pressure cooker and add 5 cups of cold water
5 add the whole onion, the black pepper, cardamom, cinnamon, *mistika*, and *shaibah*, and salt to taste
6 cook in the pressure cooker for about 45 minutes until the meat is falling off the bones then, when the pressure cooker has been opened
7 add the cooked chick peas, bring to the boil with the trotters, and remove from the heat
8 break the loaf of flat bread into pieces, and place in a deep serving dish
9 strain the stock from the trotters and chick peas and pour it gently over the bread until the pieces are sodden
10 spoon out the chick peas and spread over the sodden bread
11 pour the yoghurt evenly over the chick peas
12 remove the bits of meat from the trotters [optional] and pile them on top of the bed of yoghurt
13 fry the garlic in a small amount of butter, add it to the lemon juice, then pour over everything

to serve
- serve hot immediately
- serve with a green salad on the side

LAMB AND RICE

Lamb and rice was served in the roadside restaurants all the way down the Asir on one of our trips. Sensational as it then was after endless hours of driving, home-made *kabsa* with the optional use of vegetables is far, far superior.

for four to six people
1 kilo of lamb (chunks on the bone)
2 cups of rice
2 cinnamon sticks
6 cardamom seeds (whole)
50 grams of tomato purée
½ teaspoon of cumin
1 large onion (finely chopped)
salt and black pepper
butter
2 carrots (cut into big pieces) [optional]
½ cup of peas (podded) [optional]
2 tomatoes (chopped) [optional]

preparation
1 gently heat the butter in a pan, and brown the lamb with the chopped onion for about 10 minutes, turning all the time
2 add the cumin, cinnamon sticks, cardamom seeds and salt and pepper to taste, then
3 add the tomato purée, mix, and continue browning for 10 more minutes, still turning
4 if using the optional vegetables, add them now, mix well, and let them brown gently for a few minutes
5 add 5 cups of boiling water, bring to the boil, and allow to simmer gently for 1 hour
6 add the rice and mix – you may need to add a further 1 or 2 cups of boiling water at this stage for the rice – then
7 cook the rice and lamb gently for 20 minutes or until the rice is cooked and the liquid is all absorbed

to serve
■ serve hot in a large platter
■ serve accompanied by pickles (see pp. 123-8) and salad

LIVER WITH GARLIC

Baked liver with garlic, sliced and served with various salads and pickles, can constitute either the whole or part of a main course.

for six people
¾-1 kilo of lamb's liver (in one whole piece)
2 tablespoons of fresh parsley (chopped)
6 cloves of garlic (chopped)
butter
salt and black pepper
cayenne pepper

preparation
1 wash, drain, and skin the liver, then
2 make a deep slit almost dividing the liver in two
3 mix the chopped parsley and garlic with salt, black pepper and cayenne pepper to taste, and stuff the liver
4 generously smear the outside of liver with butter
5 place the stuffed liver in a small oven dish, cover with silver foil, and cook in a pre-heated oven (350°F) for 15 minutes
6 uncover and brown for another 10 minutes – longer if desired

to serve
■ place in a serving dish and slice the stuffed liver into 6-8 portions
■ serve hot with fresh tomato and cucumber salad, or green salad, and radishes, olives, and flat Arabic bread (see p. 115)

KUFTA BI TAHINA

MINCED BEEF WITH TAHINA

A main dish, served with plain white rice and shredded lettuce salad.

for four people

¾ kilo of beef (minced)
4 tablespoons of fresh parsley (chopped)
4-6 cloves of garlic (chopped)
1 large onion (finely chopped)
3-4 tomatoes (cut up into rings)
2 lemons
2 eggs

1 tablespoon of flour
vegetable oil (for frying)
juice of 1 lemon
¾ cup of tahina
cayenne pepper
salt and black pepper

preparation
1 put the beef, onion, garlic, and parsley in a bowl with salt, pepper and cayenne pepper to taste
2 add the raw eggs and the flour, mix well, then
3 between the palms of your hands, make small balls, ovals, or round flat patties from the beef mixture
4 heat a fair amount of vegetable oil in a large frying pan, lightly brown the balls (ovals or patties) on all sides, then place them on kitchen paper to drain off excess oil
5 now pour out most of the oil from the pan, leaving about 2 tablespoonfuls, and place over a very gentle heat
6 pour in the tahina and fry for about 1 minute, mixing all the time with a wooden spoon, then
7 very slowly, and mixing all the while, add 2½ cups of hot water to the tahina and allow to simmer gently for 1 minute, then
8 still mixing continuously over a gentle heat, slowly add the lemon juice – if the tahina curdles, remove it from the heat, add more water, and mix until the even, creamy texture reappears
9 now add a little salt and cayenne pepper, allow to simmer gently for 1-2 minutes, then remove from the heat
10 place all the meat balls in an oven dish, and cover with the tahina sauce
11 add the tomato rings as a top layer
12 cover the dish with a lid or silver foil and place in a pre-heated oven (350°F) for 20 minutes, then
13 uncover and allow the tomatoes to brown for 5-10 minutes

to serve
■ serve hot in the same dish with white rice
■ serve lemon wedges on the side to squeeze on meat as desired

MINCED MEAT KEBAB

If you use lamb, the best cut is the leg, completely boned and finely minced. A dish made and loved all over the Arab world, it is ideal for outdoor evening barbecues, served with rice, salads, *mutabbal*, yoghurt, and flat Arabic bread.

for six people
1½ kilos of lamb (finely minced)
1 large bunch of parsley (finely chopped)
2 onions (finely chopped) **or** 6 cloves of garlic
   (chopped) – do not use both garlic and onion
1 teaspoon of mixed spices
salt and black pepper
½ teaspoon of ground chilli pepper

preparation
1 place the minced meat, parsley, onion (or garlic), mixed spices, salt and black pepper to taste, and chilli pepper in a large mixing bowl, and mix really well by hand – alternatively pass all the ingredients through a meat mincer to get them well mixed
2 wet your hands with a little cold water, take a handful of the meat mixture, and knead it into 10-cm long rolls about 5 cm thick – repeat until all the meat is used up
3 thread 2 or 3 of the meat rolls onto a skewer and gently squeeze them to secure them – the meat should be sufficient for 8-10 skewers
4 light a charcoal fire, allow the flames to die down and, when left with hot embers, cook the skewers over the fire turning regularly so that the kebabs are cooked on all sides – cook for about 10 minutes or longer as desired

to serve
■ serve hot on skewers with flat Arabic bread (see p. 115), salads, and yoghurt (see p. 144), or
■ remove the meat from the skewers using a loaf of flat Arabic bread to pull it off, then arrange the kebab nicely on a platter surrounded with the vegetable [if used] and serve immediately
■ barbecue rings of aubergine, quarters of tomatoes, and slices of green pepper for show and flavour

COURGETTES WITH BEEF OR LAMB

The meat used may be either minced lamb or beef, with or without pine nuts, cooked in a thick tomato sauce and served with rice that has been cooked with a touch of tomato purée. An accompanying bowl of fresh mint, radishes, and *jarjeer* (a type of cress), makes this dish a good and wholesome main course.

for six people
10-12 small young courgettes
¾ kilo of lamb or beef (minced)
1 large onion (finely chopped)
2 tomatoes (cut into rings)
2-4 cloves of garlic (chopped)
2 tablespoons of fresh parsley (chopped)
2 tablespoons of pine nuts [optional, though
    worth having]
70 grams of tomato purée
vegetable oil (for frying)
½ teaspoon of mixed spice
salt and black pepper

preparation
1 wash and dry the courgettes, then scrape, top and tail them, and slice them each lengthwise into about four slices
2 heat vegetable oil about 1 cm deep in a frying pan over a moderate heat, brown the courgette slices to a golden colour on both sides, then remove and place them on kitchen paper to drain off excess oil
3 pour out excess oil from frying pan (keeping about 1 tablespoon), add the meat and onion, and sauté for about 10 minutes, turning all the time
4 add the garlic, parsley, salt and pepper to taste, pine nuts [if using them], mixed spices, and finally the tomato purée and continue sautéing for another 10 minutes mixing regularly
5 add a cup of water, simmer the meat mixture until the water is almost absorbed, then remove from the heat and leave aside
6 into a fairly shallow oven dish, place alternating layers of fried courgettes and meat mixture, beginning and ending with a layer of courgettes
7 top the dish with the tomato rings, then
8 pour in 1 cup of boiling water, cover with silver foil and place in a pre-heated oven (350°F) for 30 minutes

to serve
- serve hot with rice cooked with a touch of tomato purée
- serve warm with rice, or with salads and other dishes, at a buffet

LAHIM WA 'AJEEN

LAMB AND PASTRY

An open pastry that has been described as the Middle Eastern pizza, although in reality there is no comparison. It is an extremely popular dish all over the Middle East, and has become a regular feature at most large buffet parties in Saudi Arabia. Here is the recipe for about 20 medium to small ones for you to try.

for four people
dough (see below)
½ kilo of lamb (minced)
4-6 large ripe tomatoes (peeled and finely chopped)
2 tablespoons of fresh parsley (chopped)
6 cloves of garlic (crushed)
1 teaspoon of *sumac*
salt and black pepper
cayenne pepper

preparation
1 make a dough according to the recipe *'Ajeenat lahim wa 'ajeen* (see p. 112), and leave it to rise for 2 hours in a warm place
2 meanwhile mix the minced lamb, chopped tomatoes, parsley, garlic, *sumac*, and salt, pepper, and cayenne pepper to taste
3 when the dough is risen, knead it once more, and divide it into about 20 small egg-size portions
4 roll each portion into a round ball and allow them to rest for 10 minutes, then
5 flatten the dough balls with your hands (or with a rolling pin) into thin patties about 8-10 cm in diameter
6 spread each patty evenly with generous handful of meat mixture – leaving a rim of uncovered dough at the edges – and place on a lightly greased baking tray
7 cook in a pre-heated oven (450°F) for about 10 minutes, or until the dough edges look brown

to serve
■ serve hot as a main course with salads, pickles (see pp. 123-128), and yoghurt (see p. 144)
■ cool, pack, and refrigerate or freeze, then re-heat again in the oven when required

STUFFED CARROTS, TURNIPS AND CUCUMBERS

A *mahshi* (stuffed vegetable dish) which gives a choice to suit all tastes.

for six people
6 turnips (round, smooth-skinned and even-
  sized)
6 carrots (fat and short)
6 cucumbers (small and fat)
½ kilo of lamb or beef (minced)
1 cup of rice
1 onion (finely chopped)
1 tablespoon of fresh parsley (chopped)
50 grams of butter
a few bones (or 2 cups of bone stock)
2 lemons
pinch of cinnamon
salt and black pepper

preparation
1 wash and core the turnips, carrots, and cucumbers, leaving ½ cm thick shells
2 rinse the vegetables thoroughly inside and out, and drain
3 prepare a stuffing by mixing the rice, meat, onion, parsley, butter, cinnamon, and salt and
   pepper to taste, then
4 stuff each vegetable until it is almost, but not quite, full to the brim
5 if using bones place them on the bottom of a cooking pan, then
6 on top of the bones place the stuffed vegetables fairly close to each other and with their open
   ends facing upward
7 add 2 cups of boiling water, or 2 cups of stock (if using stock and no bones), sprinkle with a
   little more salt, and cover
8 bring to the boil, then allow to simmer for 40-45 minutes – adding more boiling water, if
   necessary, while cooking

to serve
■ arrange the vegetables attractively on a large platter, and serve hot with stock in a bowl on the
  side
■ serve a bowl of yoghurt (see p. 144) with 1-2 cloves of garlic crushed in it, as an accompaniment
■ serve wedges of lemon to be squeezed on the vegetables as desired

MARGOUG

LAMB WITH THIN BREAD

Margoug is served on a bed of thin bread (*ragayig*) or with freshly made dough. This version is made with bread; the alternative is far more laborious. *Ragayig* is sold in packs of 10 or 12 in the shops; it requires special baking utensils to make, so is better bought.

for eight people
1½-2 kilos of lamb (chunks, on or off the bone)
1 large onion (finely chopped)
6 very small carrots (whole, peeled)
4 very small courgettes (whole, scraped, topped,
   tailed)
4 very small aubergines (whole, with stalks cut off)
12 whole green beans, tied into 2 bundles of 6
   each [optional]
50 grams of tomato purée
4 heads of leeks [optional]
2 tomatoes (chopped)
10 whole cardamom seeds
6 whole cloves
salt and black pepper
½ teaspoon of mixed spices
vegetable oil
2-3 loaves of thin bread (*ragayig*) dried in the sun

preparation
1   heat about 2 tablespoons of vegetable oil in a large pan, and sauté the chopped onion for a few minutes
2   add the chunks of lamb and continue to sauté for 10-15 minutes, turning all the time
3   lower the heat, add the tomato purée and continue to sauté for another 5 minutes
4   add salt and pepper to taste, the cardamom, cloves, and mixed spices, and mix well
5   add boiling water to cover all the ingredients, bring to the boil, then allow to simmer for 45 minutes
6   add the carrots, courgettes, aubergines, green beans and leeks [if used], and tomatoes, and add more boiling water if all ingredients are not covered
7   bring to the boil, then allow to simmer very gently for a further 30 minutes
8   5 minutes or so before serving, pile the dried *ragayig* in a large deep serving dish
9   pour the juice of the cooked lamb and vegetables onto the bread and leave it to be absorbed, then
10 pour the vegetables and lamb onto the heap of soaked *ragayig*

to serve
■ serve immediately
■ when serving make sure that slices of *ragayig* are included as well as the meat and vegetables

60

LAMB WITH TAHINA

A Saudi dish, popular during the holy month of Ramadan.

for four people
1 kilo of lamb (chunks, on or off the bone)
1-2 tomatoes (chopped)
1 onion (finely chopped)
2-3 cloves of garlic (crushed)
1 cup of tahina
50 grams of tomato purée
2 tablespoons of grape vinegar
salt and black pepper
2 cinnamon sticks
6 whole cloves
vegetable oil

preparation
1   heat 2 tablespoons of oil in a saucepan, and gently sauté the chopped onion for a few minutes
2   add the chunks of lamb, and continue to sauté with the onion for 10-15 minutes, turning regularly so that the onions do not burn
3   add salt and pepper to taste, then add the cinnamon, cloves, and tomato purée, mix, and continue to sauté for another 2-3 minutes
4   add 2 cups of hot water, and mix
5   add the chopped tomatoes, bring to the boil, and allow to simmer gently for 30 minutes
6   meanwhile place the tahina in a bowl and slowly add the vinegar, mixing all the time with a fork to stabilize the tahina, then mix in the crushed garlic
7   pour the tahina mixture over the meat, stir, add boiling water if necessary, bring to the boil, and allow to simmer for a further 20 minutes, stirring occasionally

to serve
■ serve hot with plain rice, pickles (see pp. 123-128), and green salad

SALEEQ

LAMB AND RICE BOILED IN MILK

Saleeq comes from the word *salaqa* (boiled), and is very much a boiled dish. But it is very aromatic in spite of using only very limited foodstuffs. I think it is an exceptionally good dish.

for four people
¾ kilo of lamb (chunks on the bone)
2 cups of long-grain rice
½ teaspoon of rosemary leaves
2 cinnamon sticks
½ teaspoon of mixed spices
5 whole *hab hilu* (a sweet spice – see p. 151)
salt and black pepper
50 grams of butter
2 cups of milk (if made up from powdered milk
    use 1 cup milk powder to 2 cups water)
1 piece of *shaiba* (a lichen – see p. 153)
1 piece of *mistika* (see p. 152)

preparation
1   place the lamb chunks into a large pan along with all the spices, but no salt
2   cover with cold water, bring to the boil, then allow to simmer for about 1½-2 hours – adding water if necessary
3   remove the lamb from the stock and keep warm (it can be warmed up in the oven towards the end)
4   strain the stock and measure out 8 cups (adding water, if necessary) for the rice, which must be cooked very slowly for 45 minutes or more until all the stock is absorbed
5   add the two cups of milk to the rice, and continue cooking gently until nearly all the milk is absorbed and the rice is soggy
6   now add the salt, mix, and cook for 5 more minutes

to serve
■ pour the cooked (soggy) rice into a large serving platter, and dot with portions of butter
■ pile the cooked meat on top and serve immediately

POULTRY DISHES

Dajaj Mahshi	STUFFED CHICKEN
Firri bi Salsah	QUAILS IN TOMATO SAUCE
Hamaam Mahshi	STUFFED PIGEON
Hamaam Mashwi	GRILLED PIGEON
Kabsat Dajaj	CHICKEN AND RICE

DAJAJ MAHSHI

STUFFED CHICKEN

Chicken stuffed with rice, nuts and raisins, and generally served with salads.

for four people
1 large chicken or two small ones (keep the
   giblets)
2 tablespoons of rice
1 very small onion (finely chopped)
1 tablespoon of walnuts (crushed)
1 tablespoon of pine nuts
1 tablespoon of raisins
1 tablespoon of fresh parsley (chopped)
butter
salt and black pepper

preparation
1 wash the chicken inside and out, drain, and pat dry with a kitchen towel
2 finely chop the chicken giblets
3 heat 30 grams of butter in a small pan, add the chopped onion and fry for about 2 minutes while stirring
4 add the finely chopped giblets, then the rice, parsley, walnuts, pine nuts, raisins, and salt and black pepper to taste, mix, and
5 fry gently for several minutes, stirring continuously
6 add ¼ cup of boiling water and allow the rice mixture to cook very gently for about 5 minutes, or until the liquid is all absorbed, and remove from the heat
7 fill the chicken with the rice stuffing, and sew or hook the opening closed to stop the stuffing from spilling
8 put the stuffed chicken into a greased roasting pan, smear it outside with a little butter, rub a little salt and pepper all over, then
9 cover with silver foil and roast in a pre-heated oven (350°F) for 45 minutes
10 finally uncover the chicken, baste it with its own juice, and brown for 15 minutes

to serve
■ slice the chicken, or divide into four, and serve with hot stuffing on the side
■ serve with more plain rice if desired, accompanied by a tomato and cucumber salad

QUAILS IN TOMATO SAUCE

Quite a variety of small birds are eaten in the Arab world, and sometimes they have so little meat on them that it seems rather a shame to kill the beautiful creatures; it does not hurt quite so much if they are bought ready to cook from supermarkets. Customarily the birds are killed, plucked, cleaned, grilled and eaten on the spot. There are, however, other ways of cooking them; 2 quails per person would be appropriate for this recipe.

for four people
8 quails (fresh or frozen)
1 onion (finely chopped)
1 tablespoon of fresh coriander (chopped)
50 grams of tomato purée
butter
salt and black pepper
cayenne pepper

preparation
1   pluck and clean the birds (or wash and drain after defrosting, if frozen), then sprinkle lightly with salt and black pepper inside and out
2   heat about 100 grams of butter in a pan, lightly brown the birds on all sides, then remove them from the heat and leave aside
3   put the chopped onion into the same butter (pour some out if there is too much) and brown for a few minutes while stirring
4   add the chopped coriander, and salt, black pepper and cayenne pepper to taste and, while still browning, stir for 1-2 minutes
5   add the tomato purée, stir, and continue browning for a further 2 minutes
6   add 2 cups of boiling water, stir well to thoroughly dilute the tomato purée, bring the sauce to the boil for a moment, then allow it to simmer for a couple of minutes
7   place the birds in a row in an attractive oven dish and pour the tomato sauce all over
8   cover and cook in a pre-heated oven (350°F) for 30 minutes, then uncover and brown for 10 minutes

to serve
■ serve hot in same dish with plain rice
■ serve the birds piled on top of a mound of rice with fried almonds or pine nuts, and the tomato sauce in a separate bowl

STUFFED PIGEON

A very special dish which, apart from tasting delicious, looks quite spectacular on a dinner table. Allow one pigeon per person, and make one or two extra for they won't go amiss.

for six people

6 pigeons
½ cup of rice
100 grams beef (minced)
2 tablespoons of pine nuts
salt and black pepper
½ teaspoon of mixed spices

pinch of cinnamon
70 grams of tomato purée [optional]
1 tablespoon of parsley (chopped)
butter
1 small onion (finely chopped)

preparation

1   clean, wash and drain the pigeons, pat them dry with a kitchen towel, salt the outsides lightly, and leave aside
2   heat 50 grams of butter in a pan, add the minced meat and brown it for 10 minutes while turning
3   add the onion and brown it, still turning
4   add the rice and continue browning for another few minutes
5   add salt and black pepper to taste, the spices, cinnamon, pine nuts and parsley, mix, and brown for a further 5 minutes
6   add 1 cup of boiling water, lower the heat, and allow the water to be absorbed by the rice mixture – the rice is now partly cooked – then remove from the heat and leave aside
7   stuff the pigeons with equal quantities of the rice and meat mixture and sew or hook the openings closed
8   heat about 150 grams of butter in a deep pan and brown the stuffed pigeons all over, turning all the time, for about 15-20 minutes
9   arrange the stuffed pigeons in a large deep pan, ready to cook
10   if using tomato purée, brown the purée for a few minutes in a little of the butter in which the pigeons were browned, add 2 cups of boiling water, bring to the boil, and then pour over the pigeons to half cover them
10a if not using tomato purée, pour sufficient boiling water over the pigeons to half cover them
11   place on the stove and bring the stuffed pigeons to the boil, then allow them to simmer for about 35-40 minutes

to serve

■ serve the whole pigeons hot, with the tomato sauce or the cooking stock in a bowl on the side
■ serve with flat Arabic bread (see p. 115) and salads

HAMAAM MASHWI

GRILLED PIGEON

Pigeons grilled over a charcoal fire. Normally allow one bird per person.

for four to six people
6 pigeons
4 tablespoons of olive oil
juice of 2 lemons
1 teaspoon of rosemary leaves
salt and black pepper

preparation
1 pluck and clean the pigeons (if this has not been done already)
2 wash them well inside and out, and drain
3 with poultry shears, split the birds down the belly side and flatten them out
4 sprinkle with salt and pepper lightly on both sides, then
5 mix about 4 tablespoons of olive oil with lemon juice and rosemary leaves, smear the birds generously both inside and out, and allow them to marinade for 2 hours or more
6 light your charcoal fire and let the flame die down until you are left with a bed of red hot embers, then
7 grill the birds for about 10 minutes on each side, or until cooked to your liking

to serve
■ serve hot on a bed of rice with nuts and raisins (see *Ruz Bukhari*, p. 92)
■ serve with green salad, pickles (see pp. 123-128), and warm Arabic bread (see p. 115)

CHICKEN AND RICE

A variation on *Kabsat Lahim*, using saffron instead of tomato purée to colour the rice.

for four people
1 large chicken
2 cups of rice
1 onion (finely chopped)
2 tomatoes (chopped)
½ teaspoon of cumin seeds
6 whole cardamom seeds
1 cinnamon stick
pinch of saffron
butter
salt and black pepper

preparation
1 boil the chicken with the cinnamon stick, cumin, and whole cardamom seeds for 20 minutes in lightly salted water, then
2 remove the chicken from the stock, leave aside to cool, and then divide into 4 portions or as desired
3 drain and measure the stock to use for cooking the rice
4 infuse the saffron in ½ cup of hot water for 20 minutes, then add the infusion to the stock
5 cook the rice in the chicken stock and saffron infusion, adding hot water if necessary
6 meanwhile heat about 70 grams of butter in a deep pan and sauté the onion
7 add the pieces of chicken and then add the tomatoes, with salt and pepper to taste, and cook gently, turning regularly until the chicken pieces are cooked

to serve
■ place the cooked saffron rice on to a large platter
■ place the pieces of chicken and the tomato and onion mixture together on top of the rice
■ serve hot with pickles (see pp. 123-128) and salads

FISH DISHES

Gambari bi Salsah	SHRIMPS IN TOMATO SAUCE
Kabsat Samak	FISH WITH SAFFRON RICE
Mahaar	CLAMS
Samak bi Tahina	FISH WITH TAHINA
Samak bi Humir (Tamer hindi)	FISH WITH TAMARIND
Samak fi as Siniyah	BAKED FISH WITH VEGETABLES
Samak Magli	FRIED FISH
Sayyadiyah	FISH COOKED WITH RICE

GAMBARI BI SALSAH

SHRIMPS IN TOMATO SAUCE

Shrimps of the Gulf at their best. When fresh shrimps are available in very large quantities and at reasonable prices, make the most of it and try them with garlic and tomato purée. A quick and extremely tasty first course, or main course served with rice and salads.

for four people
45-50 fresh shrimps (washed and peeled)
4 cloves of garlic (crushed)
2 chilli peppers (finely chopped)
70 grams of tomato purée
100 grams of butter
salt

preparation
1   melt the butter in a large frying pan over a low heat
2   add the tomato purée and sauté it gently for about 2 minutes, stirring continuously with a wooden spoon
3   add all the peeled shrimps, and sauté for a further 2-3 minutes, turning continuously
4   add the crushed garlic, chopped chilli pepper, salt to taste, and sauté for a final 2-3 minutes (longer if you prefer), still continuously turning

to serve
■ serve hot with rice and green salad
■ serve as a cocktail, providing cocktail sticks for picking up the shrimps

FISH WITH SAFFRON RICE

Fish cooked with saffron rice, turned upside down and served hot with a green salad.

for four people
1 kilo of fish (small, whole fish, or fillets of large
   fish)
2 cups of rice (washed)
2 large onions (cut into rings)
5 cloves of garlic (whole and peeled) [optional]
vegetable oil
pinch of saffron (infused in ½ cup of water)
salt and black pepper
2 chilli peppers (finely chopped)
2 teaspoons of mixed spices to include:
   ground dried lime
   cumin
   cardamom
   cloves

preparation
1 clean, wash and drain the fish, and dry with kitchen paper
2 fry the fish in a generous amount of oil until just golden brown on all sides, then remove and
   leave aside
3 sauté the onions lightly in the same oil to soften – do not brown – then mix in the garlic [if using
   it], remove from the oil, and leave aside
4 place the fried fish in a layer in the bottom of a deep pan, then add the onions [and garlic], and
   sprinkle with a little salt and black pepper, and with the mixed spices
5 cover with the washed rice, and pour 4½ cups of boiling water and the saffron infusion over the
   rice – do not mix the fish and rice; keep the rice on top
6 cover with a lid, bring to the boil, then allow to simmer for 20 minutes, or until all the liquid is
   absorbed and the rice is cooked

to serve
■ turn upside down on to a large serving platter
■ serve immediately with fresh green salad and pickles (see pp. 123-128)

CLAMS

Clams are not sold in the souks of Saudi Arabia but do live in sandy shallow-water areas of the Red Sea and the Gulf. The small smooth-shelled species (cherry clams) are extremely succulent, and the larger, ribbed variety are meaty. It is a question of personal preference.

for six people
3 pints of clams (at least ½ pint per person)
4 cloves of garlic (crushed)
4 ounces of butter
a few sprigs of parsley
black pepper

preparation
1 totally immerse the clams in fresh water for an hour, then
2 put them in a colander, and rinse beneath fresh running water for about 10 minutes, occasionally mixing by hand to ensure a thorough washing, and drain
3 heat the butter in a deep pan over moderate heat, then add the clams all at once
4 stir rapidly with a wooden spoon so that they mix
5 add the crushed garlic, parsley, and lots of black pepper, and continue stirring with the wooden spoon
6 all the clams should pop open within 4-5 minutes, whereupon
7 remove from heat and serve

to serve
■ serve absolutely at once in a big bowl
■ provide finger bowls, paper napkins, and an empty bowl for shells
■ the clams are picked up with the fingers and the contents (clam, juice, garlic, and all) sucked out
■ the clams that close again as they cool can just be re-heated

SAMAK BI TAHINA

FISH WITH TAHINA

An ideal dish for almost any fish, although the tahina can overpower the more delicately flavoured types. I recommend that fillets of fish are used to avoid small bones that can be hazardous when disguised in the sauce.

for six people
1½ kilos of fish (preferably without bones)
1 cup of tahina
6 cloves of garlic (chopped)
2 onions (cut into rings)
4 tomatoes (cut into rings)
1 lemon (cut into rings)
vegetable oil
juice of two lemons
½ teaspoon of powdered chilli pepper
1 tablespoon of parsley (chopped)
salt and black pepper

preparation
1 fry the fish in vegetable oil until it is a light golden colour on all sides, then place on kitchen paper to drain
2 pour out most of the oil, leaving about 1 tablespoonful in the pan, then
3 place the pan on a very low heat and gently pour in the tahina, stirring continuously with a wooden spoon
4 add 1 cup of cold water to the tahina, still stirring, then
5 slowly, and still stirring continuously, add salt and black pepper to taste, the chilli pepper and the garlic, and last of all the lemon juice, and allow it to simmer for a minute while still stirring
6 remove from the heat – if the sauce appears lumpy or thick, add water gradually, stirring again, until it has a runny consistency
7 place the fried fish into an oven dish and pour the tahina sauce all over it
8 cover with a layer of onion rings, then a layer of tomato rings, and sprinkle with a little salt
9 cover with silver foil and place in a pre-heated oven (400°F) for 15 minutes, until it is bubbling gently, then
10 lower the oven heat, remove the silver foil and allow to brown for 10-15 minutes

to serve
■ serve hot, garnished with parsley and slices of lemon
■ serve with plain rice and green salad

SAMAK BI HUMIR (TAMER HINDI)

FISH WITH TAMARIND

This dish, best served with plain rice and salads, comes from the Eastern Province of Saudi Arabia. The tamarind here gives the fish a nice sweet and sour taste; it is also suitable to use with large freshwater fishes.

for six people
1 whole fish (white, fleshy, and about 1½-2
    kilos in weight)
1 tomato (finely chopped)
2 large tomatoes (cut into rings)
4 potatoes (cut into rings)
2 spring onions (finely chopped)
1 large onion (cut into rings)
1 cup of fresh parsley (chopped)
50 grams of butter
4 tablespoons of tamarind juice (*humir* – see
    p. 151)
salt
cayenne pepper
pinch of cumin powder

preparation
1   remove the head and tail, and clean, wash and drain the fish
2   split the fish along the length of its belly, open it out flat, and
3   place it in a greased oven dish, with the inside flesh facing upward
4   mix together the chopped spring onion, chopped tomato, parsley and tamarind, with salt, cayenne pepper and cumin to taste, and spread evenly over the fish
5   cover with a layer of onion rings, then a layer of tomato rings, then a layer of potato rings, and finally a layer of tomato rings on top, sprinkle with a little more salt, and dot the butter around
6   cover with silver foil and cook in a pre-heated oven (350°F) for 45 minutes, then
7   uncover and cook for a further 15 minutes or until the top layer of tomatoes is brown – test the flesh of fish with a pointed knife to make sure it is well cooked

to serve
■ serve hot with plain rice
■ serve with green salads

SAMAK FI AS SINIYAH

BAKED FISH WITH VEGETABLES

The fish can either be baked, or cooked on top of the stove in a baking tray, with vegetables and spices. It is served with plain or saffron rice and fried pine nuts.

for six people
1 whole fish (preferably boneless and about 1½
   kilos in weight)
1 onion (cut into rings)
3 tomatoes (cut into rings)
4-6 potatoes (cut into rings)
1 tablespoon of fresh parsley (chopped)
½ tablespoon of fresh coriander (chopped)
2 cloves of garlic (chopped)
50 grams of tomato purée
salt and black pepper
pinch of cumin
1 lemon (peeled and cut into rings)

preparation
1   remove the head and tail, and clean and wash the fish thoroughly – if you wish (although not recommended) you may fillet the fish
2   pat the fish dry with kitchen paper and sprinkle it on all sides with a little salt and black pepper and cumin
3   grease a deep baking tray, and lay the fish in the middle
4   place the onion rings on top of fish, then the tomato rings on top and around the onions, then the lemon rings, then the potato rings on and around to fill the tray
5   sprinkle with the parsley and coriander, a little salt and black pepper to taste, and the chopped garlic
6   dilute the tomato purée in 1 cup of hot water and pour over the fish and vegetables – the water level should just reach half way up the ingredients, so add hot water if necessary
7   cover with silver foil, place in a pre-heated oven (375°F), and bake for 45 minutes
8   uncover and check that the water has not totally evaporated (add a little if necessary), lower the heat, and bake for another 15 minutes
9   alternatively cook this dish on top of the stove

to serve
- serve it straight from the oven to the table
- serve with flat Arabic bread (see p. 115) and green salad

79

SAMAK MAGLI

FRIED FISH

Frying, and usually deep frying, is the most popular way of cooking fish both in Saudi Arabia and throughout the Arab world.

for four people
1 kilo of fish (filleted – it is essential to use a fish
   which has a hard white flesh such as shark,
   barracuda, or jack)
2-3 lemons
butter
a few sprigs of parsley
salt and black pepper

preparation
1 cut the fillets into finger-size portions
2 lightly salt and pepper them and squeeze lemon juice all over
3 heat sufficient butter in a large frying pan for shallow frying
4 fry the fish portions until golden brown on all sides

to serve
■ arrange the fried fish on a platter, sprinkle with a little salt, and decorate with parsley
■ serve hot with lemon wedges to squeeze on as desired

SAYYADIYAH

FISH COOKED WITH RICE

Sayyadiyah (derived from the word *sayyad*, meaning fisherman) is cooked with *qirsh* (shark) or with *Sultan Ibrahim* (red mullet) and with fried and then ground onions which give it a distinctive dark colour. It is served with tomato and cucumber salad, or with tomato and tahina salad.

for eight people
1½-2 kilos of fish (whole red mullet or shark
    steaks)
4 cups of rice (washed)
5 onions (segmented)
1 teaspoon of coriander powder
½ teaspoon of cumin powder
2 tablespoons of almonds (blanched and peeled)
salt and black pepper
vegetable oil

preparation
1 clean, wash, and pat the fish dry with kitchen towel
2 remove and discard the tails (when using whole fish)
3 cut off and keep the heads (when using whole fish)
4 heat a fair amount of oil in a large frying pan, and fry the heads until only half cooked, then
5 remove them from the pan and place on kitchen paper to drain excess oil – keep the oil for
    frying the fish
6 heat about 4 tablespoons of fresh oil in a separate pan and, while turning regularly, brown the
    onion segments until crisp, then
7 remove them from the oil and spread them on kitchen paper to dry
8 once dry, grind the onions into a coarse powder
9 put the oil in which the onions were fried into a large pan, add the ground onion, and then the
    cumin, coriander, salt and pepper to taste, and finally the fish heads
10 add 4 cups of water, bring to the boil, and allow to simmer for 30 minutes
11 now add the 4 cups of rice and 7 more cups of boiling water, mix, bring to the boil again, and
    allow to simmer for another 20 minutes, until all the water is absorbed and the rice is cooked
12 meanwhile, fry the whole fish (or fish steaks) until cooked (about 5 minutes on each side), then
    remove and place them on kitchen paper to drain off excess oil before serving
13 separately fry the almonds to a golden colour in a little oil

to serve
■ pour the rice and fish heads into a large serving platter
■ place the hot fried fish, as they are, on top of the rice
■ sprinkle with the fried almonds

VEGETABLE AND GRAIN DISHES

Faqa' (Kama')	DESERT TRUFFLES
Foul Akhdar bi Laban	BROAD BEANS WITH YOGHURT
Lubya bi Zait	GREEN HARICOT BEANS IN OIL
Kurrat bil Bayd	BABY LEEKS WITH EGGS
Magaali	FRIED VEGETABLES
Mujaddara	LENTILS AND RICE
Rijlah bi 'Adas	RIJLAH WITH LENTILS
Ruz bi Lahim wa Hummus	RICE WITH MEAT AND CHICK PEAS
Ruz Bukhari	BUKHARI RICE
Ruz Zurbiyaan	RICE AND MEAT IN YOGHURT
Sabaanikh bi 'Adas	SPINACH WITH LENTILS
Sabaanikh bi Bayd	SPINACH WITH EGGS
Turli	MIXED VEGETABLES

FAQA' (KAMA')

DESERT TRUFFLES

Red, white, and black truffles appear in the desert in the Eastern Province following the rains in November-December. There may be a bumper crop or none at all, according to the rainfall. White truffles are the most sought after and are even used to replace meat in some dishes. They can be sliced and sautéed with onions in oil or butter, then cooked with seasoning and water and made into a dip. Another popular way to eat them is to slice them and cook them with eggs. This recipe is for truffles with lamb.

for six to eight people
1 kilo of truffles
½ kilo of lamb (chunks, no fat)
1 onion (chopped)
salt and black pepper
juice of 2 lemons
butter

preparation
1   soak the truffles in cold water to get rid of the sand, scrub well, and rinse
2   peel the truffles, rinse again, then
3   cut each truffle into four sections
4   sauté the chopped onion in about 50 grams of butter until just soft, then add the meat and brown with the onion for about 10 minutes while turning
5   add salt and pepper to taste, and mix
6   add a cup of water to the meat, bring to the boil, then allow to simmer very gently for 30 minutes – add water if necessary
7   meanwhile, sauté the truffles in a little butter on their own, then
8   add the truffles to the meat, add water if necessary, bring again to the boil, and allow to simmer gently until the truffles are cooked (about 20-30 minutes)

to serve
■ serve hot with rice

84

FOUL AKHDAR BI LABAN

BROAD BEANS WITH YOGHURT

This makes a full light meal when accompanied by olives, pickles, cheese, etc. It can also be cooked with meat and served with rice as a main dish. I recommend the dish without meat.

for four people
3 cups of fresh broad beans (podded)
6 large ripe tomatoes (peeled and chopped)
1 onion (finely chopped)
2-3 cloves of garlic (chopped)
2 cloves of garlic (crushed)
1 tablespoon of coriander (chopped)
2-3 tablespoons of olive oil
1 cup of home-made yoghurt (see p. 144)
salt and black pepper
cayenne pepper

preparation
1 heat the olive oil in a deep pan, then
2 add the chopped onion, chopped garlic, coriander, and salt, black pepper and cayenne pepper to taste, and
3 gently brown the ingredients until the onions are limp and turning pink, but not burnt
4 add the chopped tomatoes, mix, and continue browning, while turning occasionally with a wooden spoon, until almost all the tomato is soft and juicy
5 add the beans and mix well – at this stage, and depending on the amount of liquid in the pan, you may need to add ½-1 cup of boiling water
6 bring to the boil, then cover with a lid and allow to simmer for 25-30 minutes
7 meanwhile add the crushed garlic and a dash of salt to the home-made yoghurt and mix well with a fork

to serve
■ serve the beans hot with generous helpings of the yoghurt and garlic, which is poured as desired over the individual servings

GREEN HARICOT BEANS IN OIL

Cooked in vegetable or olive oil and served as a cold dish, these are excellent with fish or meat.

for four people
½ kilo of haricot beans
1 onion (finely chopped)
4 large tomatoes (peeled and chopped)
2 tablespoons of vegetable or olive oil
salt and black pepper
1 chilli pepper (chopped) [optional]
1 tablespoon of coriander (chopped)

preparation
1 wash and dry, then top and tail the beans
2 chop each bean into 2-3 pieces
3 heat the oil in a saucepan, add the onions and gently sauté for 2-3 minutes
4 add the chilli pepper [if used], the tomatoes, salt and black pepper to taste, mix, and continue to sauté until the tomatoes are soft and juicy
5 add the beans, and sauté for a few more minutes, then
6 add ½-1 cup boiling water as necessary, bring to the boil, and allow to simmer gently for 30 minutes

to serve
■ serve hot or cold sprinkled with chopped coriander

BABY LEEKS WITH EGGS

Kurrat is a vegetable much like the green tops of young leeks, and is sold in bunches at all the vegetable markets of Saudi Arabia. A personal favourite of mine for a light lunch with salads.

for four people
1 bunch of *kurrat* (see p. 152)
6 eggs (beaten)
1 medium onion (finely chopped)
salt and black pepper
butter or vegetable oil

preparation
1   wash and drain the *kurrat*, then chop into lengths of about 2 cm
2   heat 100 grams of butter (or 4 tablespoons of vegetable oil) in a large frying pan, add the onions, and gently sauté them for 2-3 minutes, while stirring
3   add the *kurrat* and sauté with the onions for a further 5-10 minutes, while stirring
4   add salt and black pepper to taste, and stir
5   add the beaten eggs on top of the *kurrat* and onion, mix, and cook for 1-2 minutes stirring constantly

to serve
■ serve hot immediately with tomato salad and warm Arabic bread (see p. 115)

FRIED VEGETABLES

When served with tomato salad, pickles and spring onions, this makes a complete meal.

for four people
1 medium size aubergine
1 very small cauliflower
4 small sweet peppers (red or green, whole)
1 large courgette
4 chilli peppers (whole)
2 cloves of garlic (crushed)
juice of 1 lemon
small bunch of fresh parsley (for decoration)
vegetable oil
salt and black pepper

preparation
1 wash and dry all the vegetables
2 slice the aubergine and courgette into fairly thin rings and divide the cauliflower into pieces
3 heat vegetable oil about 2 cm deep in a medium size pan, then
4 **separately** fry the cauliflower pieces, the aubergine rings, and the courgette rings until just golden all over, remove and drain on kitchen paper
5 puncture both the sweet and the chilli peppers with a pointed knife, fry them lightly on all sides, remove and leave to drain
6 when all the vegetables are cool, place them attractively on a large flat platter and sprinkle with salt and black pepper to taste
7 add the crushed garlic to the lemon juice and [optional] pour the mixture all over the vegetables
8 decorate with parsley

to serve
■ serve cold with salad, pickles (see pp. 123-128) and spring onions
■ serve with warm Arabic bread (see p. 115)
■ home-made yoghurt (see p. 144) may be served on the side, or poured on the vegetables

MUJADDARA

LENTILS AND RICE

This can be cooked in several ways. I personally prefer the version using whole lentils and long-grain rice – a fluffy pilaff topped with as much fried onion as one likes; the more the onion the tastier the dish.

for four people
1 cup of whole (brown) lentils
1 cup of long-grain rice
1 large onion (segmented)
vegetable oil or butter
salt

preparation
1 wash the lentils thoroughly, drain, and put in a pan with 2 cups of water
2 bring to the boil, and allow to simmer for 30 minutes until the lentils are almost cooked – add boiling water if necessary
3 wash and drain the rice, add it to the cooked lentils, and mix
4 add about 2 more cups of boiling water to the rice and lentils (depending on how much liquid there is in the lentils – you need 2½ cups of water per cup of rice), add salt to taste, 1 tablespoon of oil, and mix
5 bring again to the boil, then allow to simmer gently for 20 minutes, or until all the liquid is absorbed
6 remove from the heat and leave, but keep warm
7 when ready to serve, heat about 2 tablespoons of oil (or butter) in a separate pan, add the onion, and brown to a dark golden colour

to serve
■ place the *mujaddara* on to a serving dish
■ pour the onion and oil (or butter) mixture over it – mix if desired
■ serve with yoghurt (see p. 144) or tomato salad and pickles (see pp. 123-128)

RIJLAH BI 'ADAS

RIJLAH WITH LENTILS

Rijlah (*baglah*) is a plant with fleshy green leaves similar to cress, available all year round in Saudi Arabia; it is sold in bunches rather than by weight. It is often cooked with meat and grain, or with grain only. It is also made into a green salad or added to mixed salads. This recipe of *rijlah* with lentils is for a light lunch or a side dish.

for four people
1 large bunch of *rijlah* (see p. 153)
1 cup of brown (whole) lentils
1 small onion (finely chopped)
2 cloves of garlic (finely chopped)
salt and black pepper
½ teaspoon of powdered chilli pepper [optional]
juice of 1 lemon
70 grams of butter

preparation
1 wash the lentils thoroughly, drain well and place in a pan with 4 cups of cold water
2 bring rapidly to the boil and allow to simmer for 45 minutes until the lentils are thoroughly cooked
3 meanwhile, cut off the thick stalks and wash the *rijlah* in a basin of water to get rid of sand and earth – you will need to wash it more than once – and drain
4 pick out the leaves and the tender stalks and discard the rest – you should end up with at least ½ kilo of *rijlah*
5 add the clean and drained *rijlah* to the cooked lentils, with another cup of water, salt and pepper to taste, and the chilli pepper [if used], bring to the boil, then allow to simmer for 15-20 minutes only and remove from the heat – the mixture should remain quite moist and soggy
6 heat the butter separately, add the chopped onion and garlic, and brown gently for about 5 minutes, stirring often

to serve
■ put the *rijlah* and lentils into a deep serving bowl and pour the fried onion, garlic, and butter all over

RICE WITH LAMB AND CHICK PEAS

Rice cooked with lamb and chick peas, and coloured with turmeric is a dish you can serve with pride to any number of people. It is very substantial and indeed very tasty. Though the cooking time is more than one hour, the preparation of it is very straightforward.

for six people
1 kilo of lamb (in chunks on or off the bone –
   leg is best)
3 cups of long-grain rice
4 onions (cut into rings)
1 cup of chick peas (to make a cupful after being
   soaked overnight)
2 cups of beef stock (use stock cubes if
   necessary)
100 grams of butter
salt and black pepper
1 level teaspoon of cumin powder
2 sticks of cinnamon
½ teaspoon of turmeric
6 whole cardamom seeds

preparation
1   melt the butter in a large pan, add the chunks of lamb, and brown gently for a few minutes
    while turning
2   add the onions and continue to brown for 10-15 minutes, still turning
3   add the chick peas and the stock and stir – make sure all the ingredients are covered with liquid,
    and add boiling water if necessary
4   add salt and black pepper to taste, the cumin, turmeric, cinnamon, and cardamom, and stir
5   bring to the boil, then allow to simmer gently until the chick peas are cooked and the lamb is
    quite tender – this takes at least 1 hour
6   add boiling water to make up to about 7½ cups of liquid (2½ cups of water to 1 cup of rice) and
    bring to the boil
7   add the rice, stir, lower the heat, and allow it to cook gently for a further 20 minutes, or until all
    the liquid is absorbed
8   remove the pan from the heat and let it rest for some 15 minutes before serving

to serve
■ serve hot with fresh salad
■ serve hot with yoghurt (see p. 144) and cucumbers

BUKHARI RICE

A famous recipe, using lamb or chicken. When cooked with lamb, the meat is often kept on the bone as this gives a rich tasty stock to the meal; the meat may be picked off the bone after cooking, and the bones discarded. Serve *Ruz Bukhari* as an accompanying dish to other meat and vegetable dishes, or serve it as a main meal with salad and yoghurt.

for four people
2 cups of rice (washed)
½ kilo of lamb (on or off the bone)
1 large onion (segmented)
1 tablespoon of tomato purée
4 whole cardamom seeds
1 stick of cinnamon
6 whole cloves
pieces of nutmeg (to taste)
6 black peppercorns
salt
2 tablespoons of almonds (peeled)
2 tablespoons of seedless raisins
vegetable oil

preparation
1 place the meat with 2 tablespoons of vegetable oil in a pan, and sauté gently for about 10 minutes
2 add the chopped onion and continue to sauté for a further 5 minutes, while mixing to prevent the onion from getting burnt
3 add the tomato purée, mix, and sauté some more
4 add all the spices, and salt to taste, then
5 add enough water to cover all the ingredients, bring to the boil, and allow to simmer gently for 45 minutes
6 add the rice and enough hot water to make up sufficient liquid to cook the rice, bring to the boil, then allow to simmer very gently for a further 20 minutes
7 just as the meat and rice are ready, separately heat 2 tablespoons of oil, add the walnuts, cook them to a golden colour, then remove them from the pan and leave aside
8 place the raisins in the same pan and sauté them for 2-3 minutes, then
9 return the walnuts to the pan with the raisins, mix, and remove from the heat

to serve
■ pour the rice and meat mixture into a large serving platter, with the meat piled on top
■ top it with the raisin and walnut mixture
■ serve hot with a green salad and yoghurt (see p. 144)

RUZ ZURBIYAAN

RICE AND LAMB IN YOGHURT

A rice and lamb dish cooked with yoghurt and spices.

for six people
1 kilo of lamb (cubed)
3 cups of long-grain rice
2-3 onions (cut into rings)
2 cups of yoghurt (see p. 144)
½ teaspoon of mixed spices (powdered) to
    include dried ground lime, cinnamon, black
    pepper, and *khulinjan* (see p. 152) in equal
    quantities
½ teaspoon of saffron or turmeric
vegetable oil
6 whole cardamom seeds

preparation
1   place the meat in a pan with 4 cups of water, add the cardamom seeds, bring to the boil, then
    allow to simmer for 30 minutes
2   sauté the onion rings in a large pan with a little vegetable oil until soft and light golden, then
3   remove the pieces of cooked lamb from the stock, add them to the onion and, while mixing,
    gently brown them for a few minutes,
4   meanwhile place the yoghurt in a bowl, add the ground spices, and the turmeric or saffron, mix
    well, and then add salt and mix
5   pour the yoghurt mixture on top of the lamb, and cook gently for a further 20 minutes
6   meanwhile, cook the rice in the lamb stock (adding salt to taste and sufficient water to make up
    2½ cups of liquid to 1 cup of rice) for 10 minutes only, then
7   pour the half-cooked rice with its stock on top of the meat mixture, but do not mix
8   cook the whole lot gently until the liquid is absorbed

to serve
■ pour out into large serving platter
■ serve hot with salads

SPINACH WITH LENTILS

Served with a meat course, as a vegetable or a pilaff dish.

for four people
2 bunches of spinach
1 cup of red (split) lentils
1 small onion (finely chopped)
1 large tomato (finely chopped)
1 tablespoon of coriander (chopped)
70 grams of butter
salt and black pepper
½ teaspoon of chilli pepper [optional]
juice of 1 lemon

preparation
1   wash the lentils thoroughly and drain
2   place the lentils in a pan with 2 cups of water, bring to the boil, then allow to simmer until the water is almost all absorbed
3   wash the spinach thoroughly, cut off and remove the thick stalks, and chop the leaves coarsely
4   heat the butter in a second pan, add the onions and sauté for a few minutes with salt and black pepper to taste, coriander, and chilli pepper
5   add the tomato, and sauté it with the onion for about 5 minutes, stirring occasionally; then add the spinach, and sauté for a further 2-3 minutes, still stirring occasionally
6   pour in the lentils, mix, bring briskly to the boil, then allow to simmer for 20-25 minutes
7   add the lemon juice and continue simmering for a final 5 minutes

to serve
■ serve hot, or just warm, with meat dishes

SABAANIKH BI BAYD

SPINACH WITH EGGS

This makes a good light lunch, served with bread, olives and radishes. Two eggs per person is an average serving.

for four people
8 eggs
2 bunches of spinach
70 grams of butter
salt and black pepper

preparation
1   remove the hard stalks, then coarsely chop and thoroughly wash the spinach leaves
2   place the spinach in 2 cups of lightly salted boiling water, boil for about 5 minutes, then drain well
3   grease an oven dish with a little butter and place the drained spinach into the dish
4   make 8 shallow depressions in the bed of spinach and break a raw egg into each
5   dot with butter, sprinkle with salt and pepper, and cook in a pre-heated oven (300°F) for 15 minutes – or longer if you like eggs well cooked

to serve
■ serve hot immediately

TURLI

MIXED VEGETABLES

This is but one variation of *Turli*; it can also be cooked with meat. It makes a very good light lunch with bread and pickles, and is also good with roasts of meat and chicken.

for six people
¼ kilo of green haricot beans
4 small aubergines
¼ kilo of *bamya* [okra]
1 large onion (cut into rings)
3 potatoes (cut into rings)
½ cup of peas (podded)
4 tomatoes (cut into rings)
50 grams of tomato purée
6 cloves of garlic (peeled whole)
a few sprigs of parsley
1 chilli pepper
salt and pepper
vegetable or olive oil

preparation
1   string and slice the beans in half lengthwise
2   wash, dry and cut the aubergines into thick rings
3   wash, top and tail the *bamya*
4   heat 2-3 tablespoons of oil and lightly sauté first the potatoes, and then the aubergines, and leave to one side
5   gently sauté the onions and garlic to soften, then add the chilli pepper, mix, sauté for one minute more, and remove from oil
6   in the same oil, brown the tomato purée for a minute or two, then
7   add 2 cups of water, followed by salt and black pepper, bring to the boil, and remove from heat
8   place the vegetables in layers in an oven dish, in the following order; aubergine; mixed onion, garlic, and chilli pepper; tomatoes; peas; potatoes; beans; *bamya*; (once again) mixed onion, garlic and chilli pepper; and finally tomatoes
9   pour in the tomato sauce to three-quarters of the height of the vegetables
10 cover with a lid and cook in a pre-heated oven (325°F) for 1 hour, checking that there is some juice with the vegetables at all times – add a little water if necessary

to serve
■ serve hot or just warm

SWEETS

THE LADY'S FINGERS

A traditional dessert or teatime sweet; it is also offered to guests with coffee in the mornings. It consists of pastry and syrup, and the end result of its rather lengthy preparation is delicious.

for eight people

4 cups of all-purpose flour
75 grams of butter
vegetable oil
2 eggs
pinch of salt
2 teaspoons of cinnamon

2 teaspoons of sugar
almonds (whole) or walnuts (broken)
syrup: 2 cups of sugar
4 cups of water
juice of 1 lemon

preparation

1 place the flour in a deep bowl and mix in the salt
2 make a well in the middle of the flour and break in the 2 eggs
3 add the butter and half a cup of vegetable oil, and mix well by hand
4 knead the mixture, occasionally wetting your hands in warm water, until a nice medium-soft dough is formed
5 divide the dough into four portions and, using a little flour to stop the dough from sticking, roll each portion into a ball, place it on a cloth, cover, and leave to rest for 20 minutes
6 next, using a long rolling pin, roll out each dough ball until nearly transparent, and cut out 10 cm squares with a sharp knife
7 mix the cinnamon, sugar, and nuts, and leave aside
8 place a whole almond (or a piece of walnut) and some of the sugar and cinnamon into the middle of each square, then fold two opposite sides of the square over the middle to make fat fingers, closing the two ends by pressing down with a fork
9 heat sufficient vegetable oil (about 2 inches deep) in a medium large pan and deep fry the fingers (a batch at a time) until just golden, then
10 remove, place on kitchen paper to drain off excess oil, and allow to cool
11 meanwhile make the syrup as follows:
    i. put the sugar into a deep pan, add the water, and heat rapidly, stirring occasionally
    ii. as soon as the syrup begins to boil, reduce the heat and allow to simmer gently, still stirring, for about 10 minutes
    iii. add the lemon juice, stir, and simmer gently for another 10-15 minutes, still stirring
    iv. once the syrup begins to thicken, remove it from the heat
12 now drop the fried fingers, a few at a time, into the hot syrup, and allow them to soak in the syrup
13 remove with a sieved spoon so that the excess syrup drains off, and place on a serving platter

to serve
■ serve hot as soon as they have been soaked in the syrup, or cold with coffee or tea
■ leftovers should be kept in a cool place, but not in the fridge

APRICOT PUDDING

A rather rich pudding, to be served in small quantities or eaten with warm flat Arabic bread at breakfast with tea. This makes the best possible use of *gamar id-din* (dried apricot paste).

for four people
500 grams of *gamar id-din* (see p. 151)
½ cup of sugar
10 dried apricots
10 dried plums (stoned)
2 tablespoons of raisins or sultanas
2 tablespoons of broken walnuts
2 tablespoons of almonds (peeled and broken)
50 grams of butter
2 pieces of *mistika* (see p. 152)
10 whole cardamom seeds (or ½ teaspoon of
    powdered cardamom)

preparation
1   tear the *gamar id-din* into pieces, place in a bowl with the sugar, cover with hot water, allow it to soak for 4-6 hours, and then purée it
2   wash the raisins, plums, and apricots very thoroughly; soak them in separate bowls of cold water for 1 hour, and then drain them
3   heat the butter in a deep pan, add the raisins, plums, and apricots, and sauté gently for about 10 minutes while mixing
4   add the nuts, *mistika*, and cardamom, mix, and sauté for a further 5 minutes
5   add the puréed *gamar id-din* (and 2-3 tablespoons of water if the mixture is too thick), continue cooking for about 10 minutes or so until the mixture begins to set, then
6   remove from the heat and allow to cool

to serve
■ serve as a cold dessert
■ serve as a topping for rice pudding
■ serve as a jam

APRICOT PASTE PUDDING

A chilled pudding made of *gamar id-din* (dried apricot paste) topped with your choice of nuts and spices.

for four people
200 grams of *gamar id-din* (see p. 151)
100 grams of sugar
1 tablespoon of cornflour (starch)
4 cardamom seeds (whole)
1 cup of a mixture of crushed walnuts, crushed
     almonds, raisins, pine nuts, peeled pistachios,
     and a pinch of cinnamon [all optional]

preparation
1   dilute the cornflour in ½ cup of cold water and leave aside
2   soak the *gamar id-din* with the sugar in 2 cups of boiling water for 2 hours, then blend or mash until no lumps are left
3   place the *gamar id-din* mixture in a saucepan, add the cardamom seeds, and bring rapidly to the boil while stirring
4   as soon as it boils, lower the heat and slowly add the diluted cornflour, stirring constantly
5   allow it to reach boiling point once again, then let it bubble for 2-3 minutes only; as you feel the mixture beginning to thicken, remove it from the heat
6   pour into one deep serving dish, or into 4 individual cups or bowls, and chill

to serve
■ serve chilled, topped with a mixture of nuts and cinnamon

MUHALLABIYYA

MILK PUDDING

The name *Muhallabiyya* is given to several different puddings in the Arab world, varying from ground rice pudding to a savory dish. However, all *muhallabiyya* dishes have the same look and texture, and all are served chilled.

for four people
2 cups of milk
2 level tablespoons of cornflour
2 level tablespoons of sugar
ground cinnamon
shredded coconut
crushed walnuts
raisins

preparation
1 dilute the cornflour in 4 tablespoons of cold water
2 heat the milk in a pan, add the sugar, and stir
3 when the milk comes to the boil, lower the heat, and very slowly add the diluted cornflour, stirring all the time
4 continue stirring and cooking gently for 1-2 minutes only – you will notice that it thickens quickly
5 remove from the heat and pour into dessert bowls or cups

to serve
■ serve hot (it is delicious) sprinkled with cinnamon, walnuts, coconut, and raisins, or chilled (as is the custom), with the same topping

MUTABBAG HILOU

SWEET MUTABBAG

Mutabbag means, literally, 'folded over and over'. This is a sweet dish of pastry and bananas, fried in butter on a large flat surface used especially for such dishes in restaurants. At home, make your *mutabbag* smaller so as to fit in a large flat frying pan. The home-made version is invariably thick and uneven, but is just as tasty and very well worth making.

for six to eight people
dough (see below)
4-6 bananas (peeled and cut into rings)
2 eggs
4 tablespoons of sugar
butter

preparation
1　Make 2 dough balls according to the recipe '*Ajeenat al Mutabbag* (see p. 113)
2　roll out each ball, making it into a large circle (about 50 cm) as thin as possible without tearing, and smear all over with a little butter
3　spread half the banana rings in the centre of each dough circle, and sprinkle with sugar
4　break the eggs into a bowl, whisk well, and pour onto the chopped bananas – half for each dough circle
5　fold the edges of each circle into the centre to form a square, then
6　heat a fair amount of butter, and fry the *muttabag* first one side then the other until golden brown

to serve
■ serve hot, cut into portions

QATAAYIF MAHSHI

FILLED QATAAYIF PANCAKES

Qataayif is the speciality sweet of Ramadan. It consists of small pancakes, first stuffed with nuts, cheese, or fruit, then baked or fried, and finally dipped in honey-like syrup and eaten hot. The pancakes, which can be bought ready-made by the dozen or the kilo, come in two sizes; the smaller variety are not cooked any further but are eaten with *ishta* (cream) folded into them; the larger ones, the size of a small saucer, are stuffed and cooked.

for four people
12 pancakes (about 10 cm in diameter)
4 tablespoons of broken walnuts
4 tablespoons of shredded coconut
2 tablespoons of fine sugar
1 teaspoon of cinnamon
vegetable oil for frying
syrup of sugar, water, and lemon juice

preparation
1   prepare the pancakes (if not bought ready-made) according to the recipe *Qataayif* (see p. 116)
2   mix the walnuts, coconut, sugar, and cinnamon, and place some of the mixture onto the 'uncooked' side of each pancake, then
3   fold the pancakes over to form bulging ½ circles, sticking the edges together with your fingers
4   heat a large amount of vegetable oil in a deep frying pan, and
5   gently drop in 3-4 stuffed *Qataayif* at a time, deep frying them until they are just golden brown on both sides, then
6   remove the *Qataayif* from the pan and place on kitchen paper to drain off excess oil
7   now prepare the syrup as in *Asaabi' il Sitt* (see p. 100)

to serve
■ dip the *Qataayif* into the hot syrup, give it a whirl to make sure that it has absorbed sufficient syrup, remove, and serve still warm

RUZ BI HALIB

RICE AND MILK

Ruz bi halib is, in fact, a rice pudding. It is served chilled, sometimes sprinkled with cinnamon, sometimes topped with a layer of jelly, and sometimes with syrup and nuts poured on top. It is very popular in the local restaurants of Saudi Arabia, and especially where they serve *mutabbag* and *shawerma*.

for four people
1 cup of rice (short grain, Egyptian)
3 cups of water
3 cups of milk
2 tablespoons of sugar
2 pieces of *mistika* (see p. 152) or rosewater

preparation
1 soak the rice in cold water for 1 hour, then rinse well
2 place the rice in a pan with 3 cups of water, bring to the boil, and allow to simmer until the water is almost all absorbed
3 heat the milk with the sugar (to dissolve) and *mistika* [or rosewater], pour onto the cooked rice, mix, and bring once to the boil
4 pour the rice and milk mixture into an oven dish, place in a pre-heated oven (350°F), and cook for about 15 minutes until almost all the liquid is absorbed and the top is turning golden

to serve
■ serve chilled either as it is or topped with cinnamon powder or nuts

DATES WITH SESAME SEEDS

Simple to prepare but quite a change from plain dates. Serve in small quantities with Arabic coffee or Turkish coffee before, or, even better, after a meal. Customarily one or two of these dates are taken at a time.

for ten people
20 dates (already stuffed with almonds – most
   Madinah dates are sold this way)
2 tablespoons of *sumsum* (see p. 153)

preparation
1   place the *sumsum* (sesame seeds) in a small frying pan over a low heat, and
2   roast to a golden colour, while stirring, then
3   remove and spread them on kitchen paper to cool
4   roll each date separately in the roasted sesame seeds, and arrange them on a sweet dish

to serve
■ serve with coffee (see pp. 134-5)

DATES WITH TAHINA

A sweet dish; sugar can be added when serving, if desired.

for four people
¼ kilo of soft dates
2 tablespoons of flour
2 tablespoons of tahina
½ teaspoon of fennel seeds [optional]
butter

preparation
1 remove all the stones from the dates, wash thoroughly and drain
2 cover the dates in two cups of hot water and soak overnight
3 mash and sieve the dates through a coarse colander, or pass through a manual blender
4 add the flour to the mashed dates, mix very well, then add the tahina and fennel and mix again
5 gently heat 50 grams of butter in a pan, pour the date mixture into it, and cook very gently, stirring all the time with a wooden spoon, until the mixture begins to set – it takes about 10 minutes
6 pour into a deep greased serving dish, and allow to cool

to serve
■ turn out upside down onto a flat platter
■ pour melted butter on top just before serving, as desired
■ serve in small quantities topped with cream, and sprinkled with sugar to taste

UMM 'ALI

Introduced from Egypt, 'Ali's Mother' is still made from old flat bread (*Khubz*, see p. 115) and milk with sugar and cinnamon. In Saudi Arabia it has now developed into a sophisticated dish with an exquisite taste.

for four people
3 eggs
2 cups of self-raising flour
butter
1 big handful of walnuts
1 big handful of pine nuts
1 big handful of raisins or sultanas
2 cups of milk
2 tablespoons of sugar
cinnamon
10 whole cloves

preparation
1 crack the eggs into a deep bowl and whisk with a fork
2 slowly add the flour, mixing with your hands until a smooth, hard dough is formed; cover the dough and leave to rest for 20 minutes
3 with a rolling pin, roll out the dough into a circle about 30-35 cm in diameter, and smear all over with a thin layer of butter
4 now roll up the dough circle into a tube with the buttered side on the inside, and
5 with a knife, cut the tube into 8 equal portions
6 roll each portion into a ball, cover with a cloth and allow to rest for a few minutes, then
7 with a rolling pin, roll out each ball into a round biscuit some 7-10 cm in diameter
8 heat 100 grams of butter in a frying pan and gently fry the biscuits for a few minutes on either side until they turn a light golden colour
9 line an attractive oven dish with 2 layers of biscuits, and
10 sprinkle with the raisins, walnuts, pine nuts, whole cloves, and cinnamon to taste
11 in a separate pan, dissolve the sugar in the milk, bring to the boil, then pour it over the biscuits and nuts
12 bake in a pre-heated oven (350°F) for 15-20 minutes – add hot milk if necessary so as to prevent the milk from drying up completely

to serve
■ serve hot from the same dish

PASTRIES AND DOUGHS

'Ajeenat Lahim wa 'Ajeen	DOUGH FOR MEAT AND PASTRY
'Ajeenat al Mataziz	DOUGH FOR MATAZIZ
'Ajeenat al Mutabbag	DOUGH FOR MUTABBAG
'Ajeenat Sambousik wa Burak	DOUGH FOR PIES
Ka'k bi Mahlab	MAHLAB BUNS
Khubz	FLAT BREAD
Qataayif	PANCAKES FOR QATAAYIF

DOUGH FOR MEAT AND PASTRY

This is the dough used in the recipe *Lahim Wa Ajeen* (p. 58)

for twenty portions
4 cups of flour (all purpose)
1 teaspoon of yeast
2 tablespoons of vegetable oil
1 teaspoon of sugar
pinch of salt

preparation
1   put the yeast and sugar in a cup, add ½ cup of warm water, and allow to rise for about 20 minutes
2   put the flour with a pinch of salt in a bowl, mix, and make a well in the middle
3   add the yeast-sugar liquid and the vegetable oil, and mix well by hand
4   knead very thoroughly, adding small quantities of warm water until a soft smooth dough is formed
5   cover with a cloth and leave to rise in a warm place for at least 2 hours

'AJEENAT AL MATAZIZ

DOUGH FOR MATAZIZ

The recipe for making the dumplings in *Al Mataziz* (see p. 44).

for four people
1 cup of flour (all purpose)
pinch of salt

preparation
1   place the flour and salt in a bowl and mix
2   add very small quantities of cold water, still mixing, until the dough is of a suitable consistency for kneading
3   knead the dough for a few minutes, make into a ball, cover with a cloth, and allow to rest for 1-2 hours

‘AJEENAT AL MUTABBAG

DOUGH FOR MUTABBAG

This is sufficient for 2 large or 4 small *mutabbag* (see p. 104), depending on the size of your pan.

for six to eight people
3 cups flour (all purpose)
pinch of salt

preparation
1　place flour and salt in a bowl and mix
2　gradually add small quantities of warm water while mixing and then knead until a soft smooth dough is formed
3　cover with a cloth and allow to rest for 20 minutes, then
4　knead the dough again, divide it into 2 portions, and roll each portion into a smooth ball ready to use

‘AJEENAT SAMBOUSIK WA BURAK

DOUGH FOR PIES

This pastry is for *sambousik* (see p. 29) or *burak* (see pp. 16-17) filled with cheese, meat, or spinach.

for four to six people
3 cups of flour (all purpose)
30 grams of butter (softened)
3 tablespoons of vegetable oil
1 large egg (or two small ones)
pinch of salt

preparation
1　place the flour and salt in a deep bowl, mix, and make a well in the middle
2　add the softened butter and egg(s) and mix well by hand
3　add the vegetable oil in small quantities and continue mixing thoroughly
4　wetting your hands regularly with warm water, mix and then knead really well until a malleable but firm and smooth dough is formed
5　cover with a cloth and allow to rest for half an hour

MAHLAB BUNS

A slightly sweet pastry made with *mahlab*, an aromatic grain. It is made in a longish braided shape and makes the perfect breakfast bun which can be warmed in the oven when required. Make a large quantity and keep either in the fridge for several days, or freeze and defrost as required.

to make thirty *Ka'ks*
5 eggs
150 grams of butter (softened)
1 cup of sugar
6 cups of flour (all purpose)
2 teaspoons of yeast
1 cup of milk (warm)
2 teaspoons of *mahlab* powder (see p. 152)
1 teaspoon of baking powder
pinch of salt

preparation
1 put the yeast, 1 teaspoon of sugar, and 2 tablespoons of warm water in a cup and allow to rise for 20 minutes
2 break 4 eggs into a large deep bowl and whisk with a fork
3 add the salt, butter, warm milk, yeast mixture, sugar, and baking powder, and mix by hand
4 adding flour a little at a time, mix and then knead until the flour is all used up and you have a fairly soft but smooth dough
5 cover with a cloth and leave in a warm place to rise for at least 2 hours, then
6 divide the dough into about 30 portions, make each portion into a smooth ball, and
7 using both hands, roll each ball into a 'worm' about 30 cm long
8 cut the 'worm' at one third of its length and make a 'T' with the shorter piece as the stem and the longer piece across it, then
9 braid or plait the longer cross piece of the 'T' over the short stem
10 place the braids on a lightly greased baking tray, cover with a cloth, and allow to rest for about 20 minutes
11 brush each *ka'k* with the remaining egg (beaten) and bake in a pre-heated oven (400°F) for 20 minutes or until just golden
12 remove from the oven, cool, and store in a tin, in the fridge, or in the freezer

to serve
■ serve warm with tea or coffee

KHUBZ

FLAT BREAD

Flat Arabic bread is served with every dip made in the Arab world; it is also excellent for sandwiches and is a must with kebabs. It freezes well when very fresh, and is easy to defrost by pre-heating the oven at a low temperature for about 10 minutes, sprinkling a little water on the frozen bread, and placing it in the oven for 10 minutes. You would not often need to make this bread at home, as it is very good and inexpensive to buy and is always fresh and available at bakeries and supermarkets seven days a week. However, should you find yourself wanting to make it, here is a recipe.

to make eight loaves

4 cups of flour (all purpose)
2 teaspoons of dry active yeast
½ teaspoon of sugar

½ teaspoon of salt
1-2 tablespoons of vegetable oil

preparation

1 put the yeast and sugar in a cup, add ½ cup of warm water, and allow to rise for 20 minutes
2 place the flour and salt in a deep bowl, pour the yeast mixture into the middle, and mix by hand
3 still mixing, add another 1½ cups of warm water in small quantities until all the water is used up
4 now knead the dough for about 15 minutes, intermittently wetting your hands with warm water to clear the flour from the sides of the bowl and to soften the dough as necessary, and slowly adding the vegetable oil to obtain a smooth and malleable dough
5 cover the dough with a cloth and allow it to rest for 20 minutes, then
6 divide the dough into 8 portions, roll each into a smooth ball between two hands, place on a cloth, cover, and allow to rest for another 20 minutes, then
7 with a rolling pin, roll out each ball into a flat circle of about 15-20 cm diameter
8 place the flat loaves on a cloth lightly dusted with flour, resting on a flat surface, cover well to keep warm, and allow to rise for about 2-3 hours
9 place as many loaves as possible on a large baking tray dusted lightly with flour; brush the surfaces very lightly with a wet cloth, and place in a pre-heated (450°F) oven for 7-10 minutes until they begin to turn golden
10 remove from the oven, and place on a rack or cloth to cool

to serve

■ serve hot straight away
■ cool and store in the bread bin to serve cold or warmed again in the oven

QATAAYIF

PANCAKES

Qataayif pancakes are available ready-made during the holy month of Ramadan. See under *Qataayif Mahshi* (see p. 105) for fillings and preparation for serving.

to make about 16 pancakes
1 cup of flour (all purpose)
2 teaspoons of dry yeast
½ teaspoon sugar
1 egg
vegetable oil

preparation
1   put the yeast and sugar in a cup, add ½ a cup of warm water, and leave to rise for 20 minutes
2   place the flour in a deep bowl, make a well in the middle, and break the egg into the well
3   then add the yeast and sugar mixture and begin to mix with a fork
4   slowly add 1½ cups of water while mixing, and continue to mix for several minutes to form a dough with the texture of runny cream
5   cover and leave aside to rise for 1-2 hours, then
6   heat a flat frying pan on the stove, add a few drops of vegetable oil, and wipe briskly with a kitchen paper towel
7   ladle out the pancake mixture, a large spoonful at a time, into the centre of the hot pan
8   lower the heat a fraction and allow it to cook for 2-3 minutes on one side only – when the top looks full of holes, remove it and stack aside to cool

to serve
■ see the recipe for *Qataayif Mahshi* (p. 105)

PICKLES AND PRESERVES

Murabba Balah	DATE PRESERVE
Murabba 'Inab	GRAPE JAM
Murabba Tamaatim	TOMATO JAM
Turshi Badhinjan	AUBERGINE PICKLE
Turshi Fasulya	GREEN BEAN PICKLE
Turshi Jazar wa Qarnabit	CARROT AND CAULIFLOWER PICKLE
Turshi Khiyaar	CUCUMBER PICKLE
Turshi Lifit	TURNIP PICKLE
Turshi Tamaatim	TOMATO PICKLE

MURABBA BALAH

DATE PRESERVE

Normally served with coffee; the dates are extracted from the syrup and offered to guests one or two at a time. The remaining syrup makes an excellent jam. You should use the fresh hard dates, preferably grown in Saudi Arabia, which are on the market from around June to October. It is a time-consuming but rewarding recipe; make only half a kilo on your first try.

½ kilo of fresh dates (yellow or red, before they
   begin to turn black)
70 grams of whole almonds (blanched and
   peeled)
syrup: 2 cups of sugar
       2 cups of water
       10 whole cloves
       juice of ½ lemon

preparation
1 wash and dry the dates and (using a potato peeler) peel a very thin layer of the skin from each date and immerse the peeled date immediately in cold water to stop it turning black
2 drain the dates and drop them immediately into a pan of boiling water for 1-2 minutes, then drain again and leave to cool
3 using a pointed knife, make the smallest slit in one end of the date, then push the stone through the slit with a skewer inserted from the other end
4 re-insert a peeled almond (whole or half depending on the size of the date) through the same slit
5 prepare a syrup by putting the 2 cups of water in pan with the sugar, bringing it to the boil, and allowing it to simmer gently for 15 minutes, then
6 add the lemon juice and the whole cloves, and simmer gently for about another 10 minutes
7 add the stuffed dates to the syrup and, stirring very gently but quite often, continue the simmering for a further 45 minutes, lowering the heat if it appears to thicken too fast
8 when, at the end of 45 minutes, the dates have a pinkish colour and the syrup is set, remove the pan from the heat and allow to cool
9 store the dates and syrup in an airtight jar to preserve

to serve
- serve whole nut-filled dates as a preserve
- serve as a jam

GRAPE JAM

Best made with the sweet seedless grapes of Taif. It has no preservative, and so does not keep for very long unless stored in the fridge.

½ kilo of grapes (stripped from their stalks)
½ kilo sugar
1 stick of cinnamon
1 teaspoon of lemon juice

preparation
1 wash and drain the grapes, and remove their stalks – the grapes should now weigh ½ kilo
2 place the grapes in a pan, add the sugar, the cinnamon, and 1 cup of water, and mix – stir gently so as not to damage the grapes
3 bring to the boil, and allow to simmer for about 35 minutes – skim the top when necessary
4 add the lemon juice, mix gently, and continue to simmer gently for another 35 minutes or so until ready – either measure it with a jam thermometer or do the plate test (see below)
5 remove from the heat and allow to cool
6 store in an airtight jar

to serve
- serve with salty white cheese, or
- serve with warm bread (or toast) and butter

Plate test: put a little of the jam syrup onto a small saucer and tilt it; if the syrup runs quickly the jam is not ready; if the syrup sticks it has been overcooked; if it trickles slowly you have got it just right.

MURABBA TAMATIM

TOMATO JAM

An unusual jam, but well worth making.

1 kilo of green tomatoes
½ kilo of sugar
juice of ½ lemon

preparation
1   wash, dry, and quarter the tomatoes, and place them in a large pan
2   add the sugar and 1 cup of water, and mix with a wooden spoon
3   bring to the boil, mixing gently but almost continuously, then allow to simmer gently for 10-15 minutes
4   add the lemon juice, mix, and continue simmering for another 40 minutes until ready – either measure it with a jam thermometer or do the plate test (see p. 121)
5   remove from the heat and allow to cool thoroughly
6   store in an airtight jar

to serve
■ serve with toast and butter

TURSHI BADHINJAN

AUBERGINE PICKLE

Aubergines pickled in olive oil. This is one of the richest pickles and is good enough to be served as a starter.

8-10 very small aubergines (as small and young
   as possible)
1 large handful of walnuts (broken into small
   pieces)
2 tablespoons of fresh parsley (finely chopped)
8 cloves of garlic (chopped)
3-4 chilli peppers (very finely chopped)
olive oil (best quality)
2 teaspoons of salt

preparation
1 wash the aubergines, trim off the stalks leaving the tips of the green leaves for show, and make a lengthwise incision almost from end to end, then
2 boil the aubergines in lightly salted water for about 3 minutes, remove and drain
3 place the aubergines on kitchen paper, cover with a cloth, and place a weight (such as a chopping board and a tin of flour) on them, then leave overnight to completely drain the juices
4 make a mixture of the parsley, broken nuts, chopped pepper, chopped garlic, and salt, then
5 part the incisions in the aubergines by hand and stuff the plants with the nut and parsley mixture
6 pack the stuffed aubergines into a sterile wide-mouthed pickling jar; completely fill the jar with olive oil, and cover with an airtight lid
7 leave to pickle for at least a week at room temperature

to serve
■ take out the aubergines one by one, divide into 3-4 portions, and serve

TURSHI FASULYA

GREEN BEAN PICKLE

Green beans, pickled in vinegar and salt water, are very good with meat dishes, *sambousik*, and with plain bread and cheese sandwiches.

¾ kilo of fresh young green beans
6-8 red chilli peppers
10 cloves of garlic
pickling juice: 2 cups of water
                1 cup of grape vinegar
                2 tablespoons of salt

preparation
1   wash and drain the beans, string them, and chop them in half
2   fill part of your pickling jar(s) with beans, adding the occasional chilli pepper (slit lengthwise to allow the taste to come through) and clove of garlic – repeat until the jar is full or all the ingredients are used up
3   make pickling juice by adding the salt to the water, allowing it to dissolve, then adding the vinegar – make as much as necessary but keep strictly to the given proportions
4   fill the jar(s) of beans to the brim with the pickling juice, close with an airtight lid, and
5   leave to pickle for 4-6 days at room temperature – you may need to leave it longer in cooler weather
6   store in the fridge when the pickle is ready

to serve
■ fork out a bowlful and serve
■ always return the jar to the fridge once it has been opened

CARROT AND CAULIFLOWER PICKLE

A delicious pickle, ideal as an appetizer. It is slightly sweet and sour and yet chilli hot. There is no firm rule about the proportion of carrot to cauliflower – half and half makes a good combination.

½ kilo of cauliflower
½ kilo of carrots
10 cloves of garlic
6-8 chilli peppers
pickling juice: 2 cups of cold water
      1 cup of vinegar (grape or apple)
      2 tablespoons of salt

preparation
1 peel and quarter the carrots lengthwise
2 divide the cauliflower into florets
3 place the carrot quarters lengthwise into your pickling jar(s), and intersperse with cauliflower florets to give an attractive and colourful arrangement, occasionally adding a chilli pepper (slit lengthwise to allow the taste to come through) and a clove of garlic – continue until the jar is full
4 make the pickling juice by adding the salt to the water, allowing it to dissolve, then adding the vinegar – make as much as you need but keep strictly to the measurements
5 fill the jar(s) of pickle to the brim with juice, close with an airtight lid, and
6 leave at room temperature for about 8 days to pickle
7 store in the fridge when the pickle is ready

to serve
■ serve as an appetizer, and with meat dishes
■ once the jar is opened, keep in the fridge and use as desired

TURSHI KHIYAAR

CUCUMBER PICKLE

Pickled cucumber is a good accompaniment to *hummus*, *mutabbal*, meat and cheese dishes. Only the tiniest young fresh cucumbers should be used. Once the jar is opened it must be stored in the fridge where it can keep for 6 months.

½ kilo of cucumbers (very small and fresh)
6 chilli peppers
8 cloves of garlic
pickling juice: 2 cups of cold water
                    1 cup of grape vinegar
                    2 tablespoons of salt

preparation
1 wash and dry, then top and tail the cucumbers
2 using a sharp knife, make a lengthwise slit all the way through the cucumber – but do **not** divide in half
3 place the cucumbers upright in a row in the bottom of your pickling jar(s), packing them as tight as possible and stuffing in the occasional chilli pepper (slit lengthwise to allow the taste to come through) and clove of garlic – repeat until the jar is full
4 make pickling juice by adding the salt to the water, allowing it to dissolve, then adding the vinegar – make as much as necessary but keep strictly to the proportions
5 fill the jar of cucumbers to the brim with the pickling juice, close with an airtight lid, and
6 leave to pickle for 3-4 days at room temperature
7 store in the fridge when the pickle is ready

to serve
■ take out cucumbers as desired, divide each into 4 long sections, and serve
■ always return the jar to the fridge once it has been opened

TURNIP PICKLE

Make a small quantity the first time; when making more (as you soon will) you can adjust the proportions as desired. There is no preservative in the recipe, so do not make it in massive quantities even though it can be stored in the refrigerator for 6-8 months or so after pickling. It is best made in small jars so that it is finished quickly whilst still nice and crisp.

1 kilo of turnips
8 whole chilli peppers
10 cloves of garlic
a few drops of edible food colouring (normally red)
pickling juice: 2 cups of cold water
          1 cup of vinegar (grape or apple)
          2 tablespoons of salt

preparation
1   wash the turnips thoroughly, drain, then top and tail them – do not peel
2   divide the turnips lengthwise into 4-6 sections
3   place a few bits of turnip in your pickling jar(s), then add a few cloves of garlic and 2-3 chilli peppers (slit lengthwise to allow the taste to come through) – repeat until the jar is full
4   make pickling juice by adding the salt to the water, allowing it to dissolve, then adding the vinegar – make as much as you need but keep strictly to the measurements
5   add food dye to the pickling juice, stir, and then fill the jar(s) of turnips to the brim, close with an airtight lid, and
6   leave at room temperature for 5-6 days to pickle
7   store in the fridge when the pickle is ready

to serve
■ serve with most meals, and especially soups
■ once the jar is opened, keep in the fridge and use as desired

TOMATO PICKLE

If you grow tomatoes at home, this is an ideal way to make use of the green tomatoes that you pick to thin the crop.

12-15 small hard green tomatoes
8 red chilli peppers
10 cloves of garlic
pickling juice: 2 cups of water
                1 cup of grape vinegar
                2 tablespoons of salt

preparation
1   wash and dry the tomatoes, then
2   using a sharp knife, make 4 short vertical incisions in each tomato
3   place the tomatoes tightly in layers in your pickling jar(s), stuffing the occasional chilli pepper (slit lengthwise to bring out the flavour) and clove of garlic between, until the jar is full or the ingredients have been used up
4   make pickling juice by adding the salt to the water, allowing it to dissolve, then adding the vinegar – make as much as you need but keep strictly to the measurements
5   fill the jar of tomatoes to the brim with the pickling juice, close with an airtight lid, and
6   leave to pickle for about a week at room temperature
7   store in the fridge when the pickle is ready

to serve
■ divide the tomatoes into 4 sections, fill a bowl, and serve
■ serve with cheese dishes
■ always return the jar to the fridge once it has been opened

AM
1984

DRINKS

'Asir Habhab	WATERMELON JUICE
'Asir Rumman	POMEGRANATE JUICE
Gahwa	TURKISH COFFEE
Gahwa 'Arabiyah	ARABIC COFFEE
Laban	YOGHURT DRINK
Sahlab	HOT MILK AND RESIN DRINK
Sharab Gamar id-din	APRICOT PASTE DRINK
Sharab Humir (Tamer hindi)	TAMARIND DRINK
Sharab il Zabib	RAISIN JUICE
Sharab Laymoun	LEMONADE
Shay bi Na'na'	MINT TEA

WATERMELON JUICE

A most refreshing drink in hot weather; chilled, and sprinkled with a little fresh chopped mint is the best way to serve it. Use slices of ripe watermelon with flesh a pinkish red to deep red colour. The amount of juice obtained will depend on the ripeness of the melon.

ripe watermelon (cut into slices)
mint (chopped very finely)

preparation
1   peel the watermelon slices, remove all the seeds, and cut up into chunks
2   pass the chunks through a hand liquidizer, or an electric fruit extractor, and collect the juice in a jug
3   chill

to serve
■ pour into individual glasses, sprinkled with a little mint to taste

POMEGRANATE JUICE

A healthy drink, served in most juice shops, and a speciality of Taif. One very large pomegranate should produce enough juice to fill 1 glass. It can be quite sweet, so for those who do not have a sweet tooth mix 3 sweet pomegranates and 1 sour pomegranate to get a sharper taste, or alternatively add a few drops of lemon juice.

1 large pomegranate (sweet) per person

preparation
1   using a sharp knife, slice the skin off the top of the pomegranate, taking care not to cut too low and so damage the pearly seeds inside
2   make 4 shallow vertical cuts in the skin as if peeling an orange, and
3   pull the whole fruit apart in 4 sections
4   carefully pick out the seeds, removing all the thin yellow pith inside which is very bitter, and
5   pass the seeds, a handful at a time, through a manual liquidizer or an electric fruit extractor, and collect the juice in a jug
6   chill

to serve
■ serve in individual glasses
■ strain as you pour into glasses (if desired)

TURKISH COFFEE

Though Turkish, this is made in almost exactly the same way throughout the Middle East. To my mind a meal is never complete without this coffee, accompanied by any of the sweet Arabian puddings and desserts. The coffee beans are freshly roasted and ground in most reputable coffee shops in Saudi Arabia, and come as light, medium dark and dark, with or without cardamom. You need the traditional coffee pot and the dainty small cups with their saucers for making and serving this coffee. It can be made (1) without sugar and called *Sada*, (2) with ½ level teaspoon of sugar per cup and called *Madhbout*, or (3) with 1 teaspoon or more sugar and called *Hilou*.

for *madhbout*
traditional coffee pot (preferably brass – they
   come in 1 to 10 cup sizes)
traditional coffee cups (small with saucers)
freshly ground coffee
sugar

preparation
1   into the appropriate coffee pot put one coffee cup of water for each cup to be served
2   place on heat and add ½ teaspoon of sugar for each cup
3   when the water is about to boil, remove the pot from the heat, add 1 heaped teaspoon of coffee per cup, and stir well
4   return the pot to the heat (and don't take your eyes from it, as it tends to boil and spill before you know it), allow it to come to the boil and remove immediately – repeat this 3 times without ever letting the coffee bubble away, then stir the top once or twice, and remove completely from the heat

to serve
■ serve immediately by placing a bit of the coffee skim in each cup with a teaspoon, then filling the cups so that all the cups have some skim (*wijih*) on top
■ serve accompanied by slices of something sweet like *halwa* with pistachio nuts
■ it is customary to make one or two cups extra for topping up those who are fond of this coffee

GAHWA 'ARABIYAH

ARABIC COFFEE

Arabic coffee can be prepared in various ways, but always contains more cardamom than coffee, and no sugar. It is the traditional welcoming drink served on every truly Arabic occasion such as weddings, receptions, gatherings, meetings and camel races. It is served almost immediately to the guests on arrival, usually before a meal. It should be served from the traditional pot (*dallah*) into the very small Arabic coffee cups (without handles), in small quantities of about half a cup at a time, and passed round anticlockwise beginning with the senior guest. The server then goes round with the pot to refill any cup that is empty, and this he will do until the guest gently wobbles his cup (always drunk from the right hand) to indicate that he has had enough. It is customary to take 2-3 cups; more than 3 would be a little greedy, less than 2 not quite polite.

1 level tablespoon of Arabic coffee (sold as such
  in all good coffee shops)
2 level tablespoons of cardamom (coarsely
  ground)
2 cups of water

preparation
1 put the coffee in a pan and warm it on a low heat for a few seconds, mixing with a spoon
2 add the water, bring to the boil, and boil for 3-4 minutes
3 pour the boiled coffee through a filter into the Arabic coffee pot (*dallah*), and
4 add the ground cardamom
5 return the pot to the heat, bring to the boil once more, then allow to gently simmer for about 20 minutes

to serve
■ plug the spout of the coffee pot with palm fibre to filter the coffee as it is poured
■ serve with the coffee pot in the left hand and the cups in the right hand at all times

LABAN

YOGHURT DRINK

Watered down yoghurt, called *laban* in Saudi Arabia, is used as an accompanying drink to peppery hot dishes in many countries, including the entire Middle East, where hot food is habitually served; it is often known by other names such as *Ayran* or *Laban wa mayya*. *Laban* can be bought ready prepared in all supermarkets of the Kingdom, but you may prefer to make your own.

Laban can be served straight as a cooling drink, or with kebabs and rice dishes; it is also good with a sprinkle of salt and a sprinkle of dried mint – I personally recommend that at least salt be added.

for four glasses
2 cups of home-made yoghurt (see p. 144)
8 cubes of ice, or 2 cups of water
1 teaspoon of crushed dried mint
salt

preparation
1   mix the yoghurt with a fork to liquidize
2   add the cubes of ice (or the water) and mix well
3   add salt to taste
4   if using ice only, wait until it has melted a little before serving – if using water only, place in the fridge to chill
5   add the mint just before serving, and mix

to serve
■ serve really chilled in tall glasses
■ serve with meat, chicken, and vegetable dishes, kebab dishes, and most definitely with rice dishes

HOT MILK AND RESIN DRINK

The resin *sahlab* produces a delicious aromatic drink, adorned with nuts.

for four cups
4 cups of milk
2 tablespoons of sugar (or to taste)
about 4 teaspoons of *sahlab* powder (see p. 153)
ground ginger or cinnamon powder
2 tablespoons of crushed walnuts

preparation
1   dissolve the sugar in the milk, bring to the point of boiling, and lower the heat
2   gradually add *sahlab* powder until the milk begins to thicken, then remove from heat
3   pour into cups

to serve
■ sprinkle with ginger or cinnamon
■ sprinkle with crushed walnuts
■ serve hot

APRICOT PASTE DRINK

A refreshing sour-sweet chilled drink made from *gamar id-din* (dried apricot paste) which is sold in all supermarkets and groceries in Saudi Arabia and looks rather like an orange sheet packed in orange cellophane.

to make four glasses
200 grams of *gamar id-din* (see p. 151)
3 cups of water
sugar to taste [optional]

preparation
1   take the *gamar id-din* and cut it into small pieces
2   put the pieces in a jug, add the water, stir, and leave to dissolve for several hours
3   if necessary put the mixture in a blender to finish off the dissolving process, then sieve into another jug, and chill
4   if sugar is desired, add it and mix before chilling

to serve
■ serve chilled in individual glasses

SHARAB HUMIR (TAMER HINDI)

TAMARIND DRINK

Served chilled, and flavoured with rosewater if desired. Though tamarind is itself quite sour, lemon juice is added to enhance the flavour.

for one jug
½ kilo of tamarind (see *Humir* – p. 151)
juice of 1 lemon
1 cup of sugar
rosewater [optional]

preparation
1 wash the tamarind thoroughly, drain it, and then soak it overnight in a deep bowl in enough cold water (6 cups at least) to cover
2 strain the tamarind through a fine wire sieve, or through muslin cloth, and discard the pulp
3 dilute the sugar in 1 cup of water and add it to the tamarind,
4 add the lemon juice and rosewater [if used], stir, and chill

to serve
■ serve chilled in glasses

RAISIN JUICE

A sweet drink made by soaking seedless raisins and sprinkling with cinnamon.

for two glasses
1 cup of seedless raisins
pinch of cinnamon
2 cups of water

preparation
1   wash the raisins thoroughly, drain, then soak in 2 cups of cold water for 4-6 hours (or overnight)
2   place the raisins and their juice in a pan over a moderate heat and cook very gently for 30 minutes or so – the raisins should be quite mushy, so add a little water if too much evaporates
3   pass through a manual liquidizer or put through a blender, then
4   strain through a wire sieve
5   chill

to serve
■ serve chilled in individual glasses, with a sprinkle of cinnamon to taste

SHARAB LAYMOUN

LEMONADE

Lemonade with rosewater. Use freshly squeezed lemons and sugar to taste.

per glass
juice of 1 large lemon
sugar
a few drops of rosewater

preparation
1   add the sugar (2 teaspoons or to taste) to ¾ of a glass of water and start to dissolve it
2   add the lemon juice, and stir
3   chill or add cubes of ice

to serve
■ add a few drops of rosewater per glass

140

SHAY BI NA' NA'

MINT TEA

The most refreshing of drinks, even in the middle of a boiling hot day. It settles the stomach after a heavy meal and can also be taken as a general palliative to all ills.

for six cups
4 teaspoons of tea (non-aromatic)
1 handful of mint sprigs (washed and drained,
  leaves and all)
4-6 teaspoons of sugar

preparation
1 put the tea and sugar in a heated teapot (the sugar may be added later, on serving)
2 bring 6 cups of water to the boil, add to the pot, stir, and allow to settle
3 add the mint (complete sprigs)
4 bring the teapot to the boil, then
5 put aside to brew for 5 minutes

to serve
■ serve hot in small glasses

YOGHURT

YOGHURT

Since so many of the dishes require yoghurt, and home-made at that, I give here my own way of making it – a recipe which has hardly ever failed me.

To make yoghurt you need milk and a starter. Powdered whole milk is excellent when fresh is not available, and ordinary commercial yoghurt can be used as a starter for the first time; when you get your own yoghurt going always keep ½ a cup in the fridge to use as the next starter. Yoghurt is best made in earthenware vessels as these hold the temperature better; pyrex dishes, however, are quite adequate. It keeps fresh in the fridge for days, and when not really fresh enough for eating it is still good for cooking – as long as it has not actually gone off.

1 pint of milk
1 tablespoon of yoghurt starter

preparation
1   put the milk into a pan, bring to the boil (it must reach boiling point), remove from the heat and pour into the earthenware or pyrex container in which it is going to set
2   allow the milk to cool for about 20 minutes until, on dipping your finger in it, you can bear the heat up to the count of ten, then
3   with no further delay, spoon some milk into a cup containing the starter (yoghurt), give it a stir, pour back into the milk, and stir
4   cover with a lid and place the container on top of a folded towel in a warm corner
5   cover with a large towel, a sweater, or an old blanket, and
6   do not move it for 6 hours (or overnight), then
7   uncover and place in the fridge to cool before eating

to serve
■ serve cold, plain, with the recommended dishes
■ serve for breakfast, with meals, or as a drink

LABNAH

DRAINED YOGHURT

Labnah, drained home-made yoghurt, keeps for months if salted and stored in olive oil. A handy instant dip to cheer the soul.

yoghurt (1 to 100 pints is all the same)
a clean cloth sack (fine cotton or linen)

preparation
1   pour as much yoghurt as you have (the more the better) into the cloth sack
2   gather the open end of the sack, tie it tightly, and suspend it from a tap over the sink
3   allow it to drain for about 2 days
4   when it is obvious that there is no more water to drain, remove the sack and empty the contents into a bowl

This is now *labnah*, ready to eat, but to store for any length of time, or when made in large quantities, continue as follows:

salt
olive oil
cayenne pepper
thyme leaves [optional]
storage jar

preparation
5   add salt* (approximately ½ teaspoon per cupful of *labnah*), mix well, then
6   roll into balls (the size of large marbles) between your palms, wetting the palms with a touch of olive oil
7   drop the balls into a storage jar (of appropriate size) and
8   cover totally with olive oil
9   cover with thyme leaves [optional], then with a lid and store in a cool place. (Although it is usual to place thyme leaves on top before covering with the lid, thyme is a very aromatic herb; I don't recommend it unless you really like the taste.)

*it is usual to add cayenne pepper along with the salt, but this can be added as desired when taking out *labnah* balls to eat

WAYS TO SERVE YOGHURT

for breakfast
- chilled, absolutely plain
- chilled, with honey
- chilled, with chopped fruit such as bananas, apples, or grapes
- chilled, sprinkled with sugar
- chilled, with cereals (instead of milk)

with meals
- plain and chilled, with almost any pilaff, stuffed vegetables, *kubbah*, or spiced pastry dishes
- chilled, adding a clove of chopped garlic per cup of yoghurt, with fried aubergines and marrows

as a drink
- chilled, liquidized with about one third ice and a sprinkle of salt – this is called *laban* or *ayran* (see p. 136) and is good with a sprinkle of mint on top

as a dip using *labnah*
- *labnah* with salt, olive oil, and a touch of chilli pepper
- *labnah* with finely chopped onion, olive oil, salt, and chilli pepper
- *labnah* with garlic, salt, chilli pepper, and olive oil

HERBS, SPICES, OTHER INGREDIENTS

As su'd	GALINGALE	*Kurrat*	'LEEK'
Baqlah	SPINACH NUTS	*Kuzbarah*	CORIANDER
Bagdunis	PARSLEY	*Lawz*	ALMONDS
Basal	ONION	*Loumi*	DRIED LIMES
Bhar	SPICE	*Mahlab*	BLACK CHERRY STONE KERNEL
Bhar hilu	SWEET SPICE		
Bharat	SPICES	*Maramiyah*	SAGE
Burghul	CRACKED WHEAT	*Mistika*	MASTIC
Filfil ahmar	CAYENNE PEPPER	*Na'na'*	MINT
Filfil hilu	PAPRIKA	*Rayhan*	BASIL
Gamar id-din	APRICOT PASTE	*Rijlah*	SPINACH NUTS
Girfah	CINNAMON	*Sahlab*	ORCHIS PLANT TUBERS
Hab hilu	SWEET SPICE	*Samsaq 'itrah*	MARJORAM
Habb	HUSKED WHEAT KERNELS	*Shabth*	DILL
		Shaiba	MOSSY TREE LICHEN
Hasa il-ban	ROSEMARY	*Shummar*	FENNEL
Hayl	CARDAMOM	*Snawbar*	PINE NUTS
Humir	TAMARIND	*Summaq*	SUMAC
Hummus	CHICK PEAS	*Sumsum*	SESAME SEEDS
Iklil il Jabal	ROSEMARY	*Tahina*	SESAME SEED PASTE
Jawzat at tib	NUTMEG	*Tamer hindi*	TAMARIND
Kabsh Kurunful	CLOVES	*Thawm*	GARLIC
Kammun	CUMIN	*Waraq il ghar*	BAY LEAVES
Karawya	CARAWAY	*Za'atar*	THYME
Khulinjan	GALINGALE	*Za'faran*	SAFFRON
Kurkum	TURMERIC	*Zanjabil*	GINGER

INTRODUCTION

HERBS AND SPICES are an essential part of Saudi cooking and used in greater variety than one would imagine; this, I believe, is due to the fact that spices were once used for trading. You will find, in the shops of the spice market (*souk*) as well as in every Saudi kitchen, spices stored both separately and also variously mixed ready for specific foods such as soups, rice dishes and meat dishes. Mixed spices are used ground or whole depending on the recipe; when used whole, the spice mixture is wrapped in gauze-like material to form a bouquet garni, which is removed from the dish before serving.

It is well worthwhile visiting a herb and spice shop and stocking up with these truly aromatic and flavour-filled additives. It must be remembered, however, that, apart from cardamom seeds, all whole herbs and spices should be thoroughly washed in cold water, drained, and spread out to dry before being mixed and stored.

AS SU'D
See *Khulinjan*

BAQLAH
See *Rijlah*

BAGDUNIS
Parsley grows well in Saudi Arabia and is used extensively in salads, with cooked foods, and as a garnish for meats, dips and fish. Almost invariably fresh green (rather than dried) leaves are used

BASAL
Onions, both green or spring onions and dry onions, are used extensively; raw and cooked are equally popular. Spring onions are served on the table with most dishes

BHAR
Singular of *Bharat*

BHAR HILU
See *Hab hilu*

BHARAT
A general word for spices, commonly used to mean mixed spices, which can vary from one mixture to another. The contents are indicated on the wrapping, and they may be whole or ground

BURGHUL
Cracked wheat is very popular in the Middle East. It has been cooked before cracking and so can be eaten without further cooking as in *Taboullah*

FILFIL AHMAR
Though this generally refers to hot red chilli pepper, whole or powdered, it can also mean cayenne pepper

FILFIL HILU
Paprika, which is used as a garnish for dips

GAMAR ID-DIN
A paste made of cooked apricots; unique to the Middle East, although it can now be bought all over the world. It is one of the specialities of Ramadan, and it is common to break the Ramadan fast with a drink of *Sharab Gamar id-din*

GIRFAH
Cinnamon is used in both stick and powder form. It is good in savouries, sweets and pastries

HAB HILU
Sweet spice. It resembles black peppercorns and is used for its sweet-smelling effect in soups

HABB
Husked wheat kernels

HASA IL-BAN
Rosemary; commonly used in its dry form with lamb

HAYL
Cardamom is used very extensively in Saudi cooking. It may be whole, or coarsely or finely ground. It gives an aroma to meat dishes, is excellent on rice, and is essential in Arabic coffee. The taste is an acquired one, and can be overwhelming to a novice

HUMIR
Tamarind (Indian dates), the pods of the tropical tamarind tree. Used with fish, meat, and vegetable dishes and most popular as a syrupy drink

HUMMUS
Chick peas, or Garbanzo beans, should be soaked overnight and cooked for at least 1 hour before being used for making *Hummus bi tahina*, or adding to vegetable and meat dishes

IKLIL BI JABAL
See *Hasa il-ban*

JAWZAT AT TIB
Nutmeg; available whole or ground from all Saudi spice shops

KABSH KURUNFUL
Cloves are normally used whole with meat dishes and sweets to impart an aromatic flavour

KAMMUN
Cumin is used in both seed and powder form for fish and egg dishes. Use it according to taste as it is quite strong

KARAWYA
Caraway, used dry in salads and sweets, and also in pastry

KHULINJAN
Galingale, a member of the ginger family, is a very aromatic root. It is used with meat dishes and almost all meaty soups

KURKUM
Turmeric, a strong yellow coloured spice with a mild aroma, is at times a substitute for saffron for colouring rice dishes

KURRAT
A plant from the leek family for which I have found no English equivalent. Young leek leaves can be substituted for it

KUZBARAH
Coriander, which is a member of the parsley family, is used extensively both fresh and dry. The taste is again an acquired one

LAWZ
Almonds are very popular in rice and meat or chicken dishes, as well as for garnishing sweets. To blanch and peel them, place them in boiling water for a minute, then allow them to cool; they will pop out quite easily

LOUMI
Dried whole limes, which are bought as such in Saudi Arabia. Dry your own by rapidly boiling them for 3 minutes, then drain and dry in the sun until completely dehydrated. They have to be grated or pounded to a powder when used, and give a delicious, sour flavour. Whole *loumis* can be dropped in some dishes, but should not be eaten when cooked

MAHLAB
An aromatic kernel obtained from black cherry stones and used in its powder form for spicing pastry. It is quite expensive so should be used sparingly. You have to grind the kernels yourself as it is never sold ground

MARAMIYAH
Sage, used for making a drink similar to tea; good for all ills

MISTIKA
Mastic, a resin from a small evergreen tree, is used with meat, chicken, and trotters. It is quite aromatic in small quantities, but can be quite bitter if used generously. Make sure you buy the cooking 'mistika' and not the chewing-gum version

NA'NA'
Mint is used extensively in Saudi cooking. It is generally used green, and only occasionally dry or powdered

RAYHAN
Basil grows wild in Saudi Arabia. The local version has beautiful flowers and very aromatic, coarse green leaves. It should be used sparingly

RIJLAH
A vegetable related to cress with fleshy green leaves and a gritty texture. It is sometimes referred to as 'spinach-nuts' in the Mediterranean. Spinach can be used as a substitute

SAHLAB
A powder from tubers of the orchis plant, which becomes gelatinous when brought to the boil with milk. Often cornflour is used as a poor substitute in making the *Sahlab* drink

SAMSAQ 'ITRAH
Marjoram

SHABTH
Dill is available fresh all the year round and is used for savouries, salads and pickles

SHAIBA
A mossy tree lichen, black gray in colour; the word *Shaiba* means 'old man'. It is used in soups and stews for its sweet aromatic effect. As bought in the spice souk, one or two pieces are enough in a recipe

SHUMMAR
Fennel, used for pastry and sweets

SNAWBAR
Pine nuts are used in meat and rice dishes, and in sweets. They are imported and expensive; but exquisite

SUMMAQ
Sumac is sold already ground; added to meat it imparts a lemony, sour taste and a red colour. It is derived from the red berries of the plant called 'Tree of Heaven'

SUMSUM
Sesame seeds, roasted to a light golden colour, are used whole in pastries, sweets, and for coating dates

TAHINA

Tahina, produced from sesame seeds, is without substitute; it is an oily gray-white paste with a distinctive smell and a unique flavour. It is now available in jars and tins all over the world as *Tahina* or *Tahini*. Tahina should not be pre-mixed with anything when used for cooking, so do not buy Tahina Sauce as this is a pre-mixed product

TAMER HINDI

See *Humir*

THAWM

Garlic is essential in Saudi cooking, where it is used with cooked meals and salads. It is permitted, up to a point, to use it according to taste, but it must never be omitted when making *Hummus bi Tahina*

WARAQ IL GHAR

Bay leaves used for flavouring meat

ZA'ATAR

Thyme is a strong herb, but is excellent with *Labnah* and salty white cheeses. It is often mixed with various herbs and spices and served with bread and olive oil

ZA'FARAN

Saffron, which is imported and expensive, is used with rice and meat. It is aromatic and colourful, and is a must when recommended (*Kurkum* will do as a substitute)

ZANJABIL

Ginger is available dry at all times and used in dry powder form in sweets. Fresh ginger, too, has recently arrived on the supermarket shelves

ENGLISH INDEX OF RECIPES

Index entries are listed alphabetically. Entries are listed generically (e.g. soups, meat dishes, fish dishes) in the contents page on pp. 4-7.

ARABIC INDEX OF RECIPES